#CharlestonLife

A COFFEE TABLE PHOTOGRAPHY BOOK BY LEEANN NEUMANN

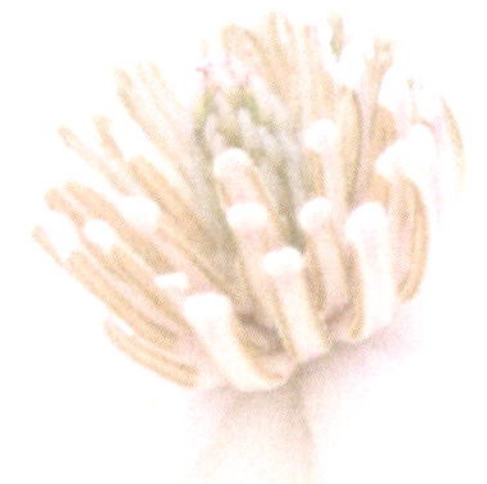

ISBN: 979-8-9938840-1-1

Edition: 001

This is a self-publication. All images, text, page and cover designs are the work of LeeAnn Neumann.

Artist Statement

I created this publication to share beauty in nature and in our surroundings that may otherwise go unseen. Whether you're native to the lowcountry, transplanted here, love to visit, or even hope to visit someday — these images were captured for you. Our lifestyles may not always allow us to experience these nature-filled moments that exist in real life every single day. The moments happening in between moments.

I hope you find a breath of fresh air here.
A moment of pause and a moment of peace.
A refresh and a reset.

Namaste,

LeeAnn

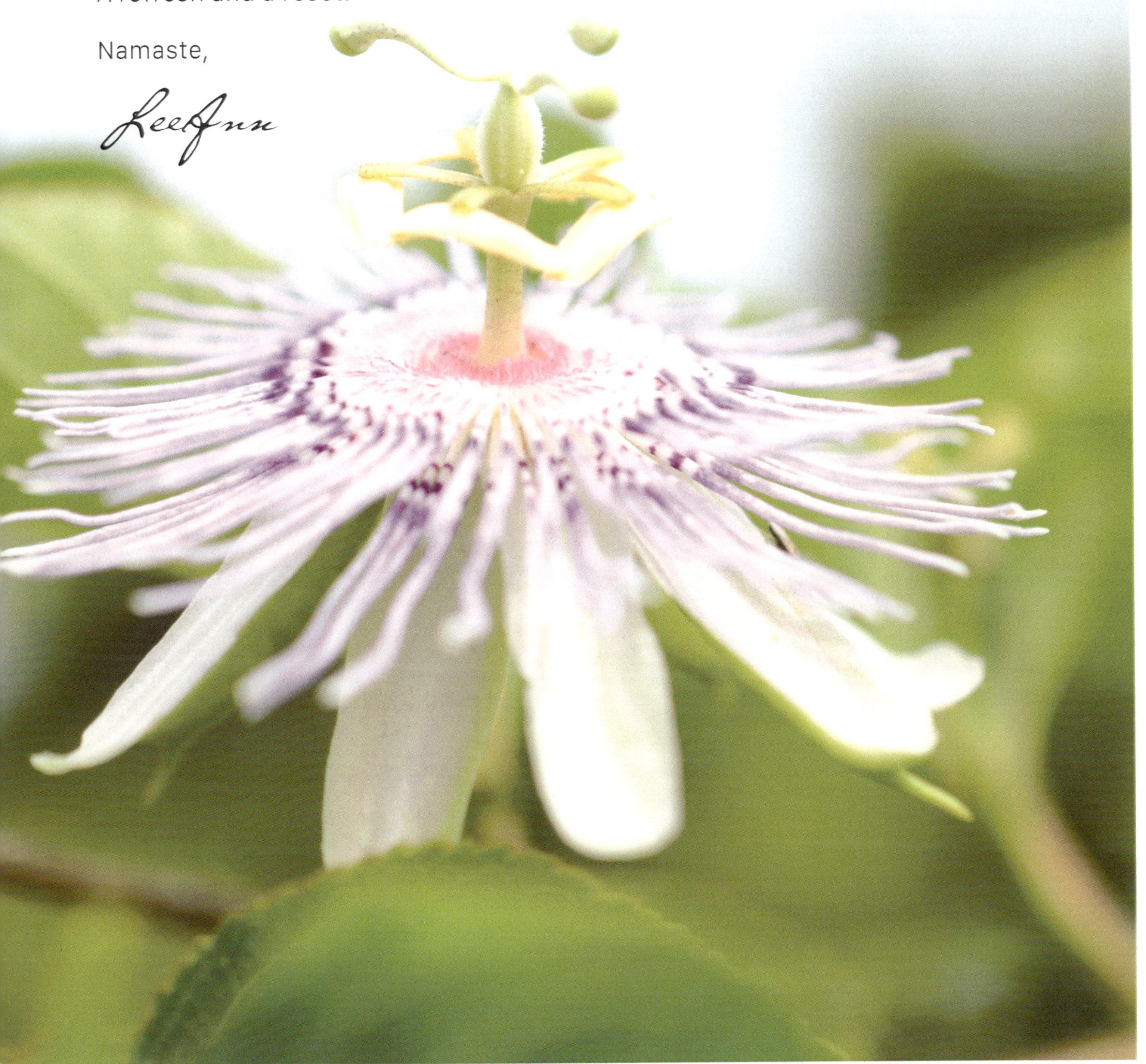

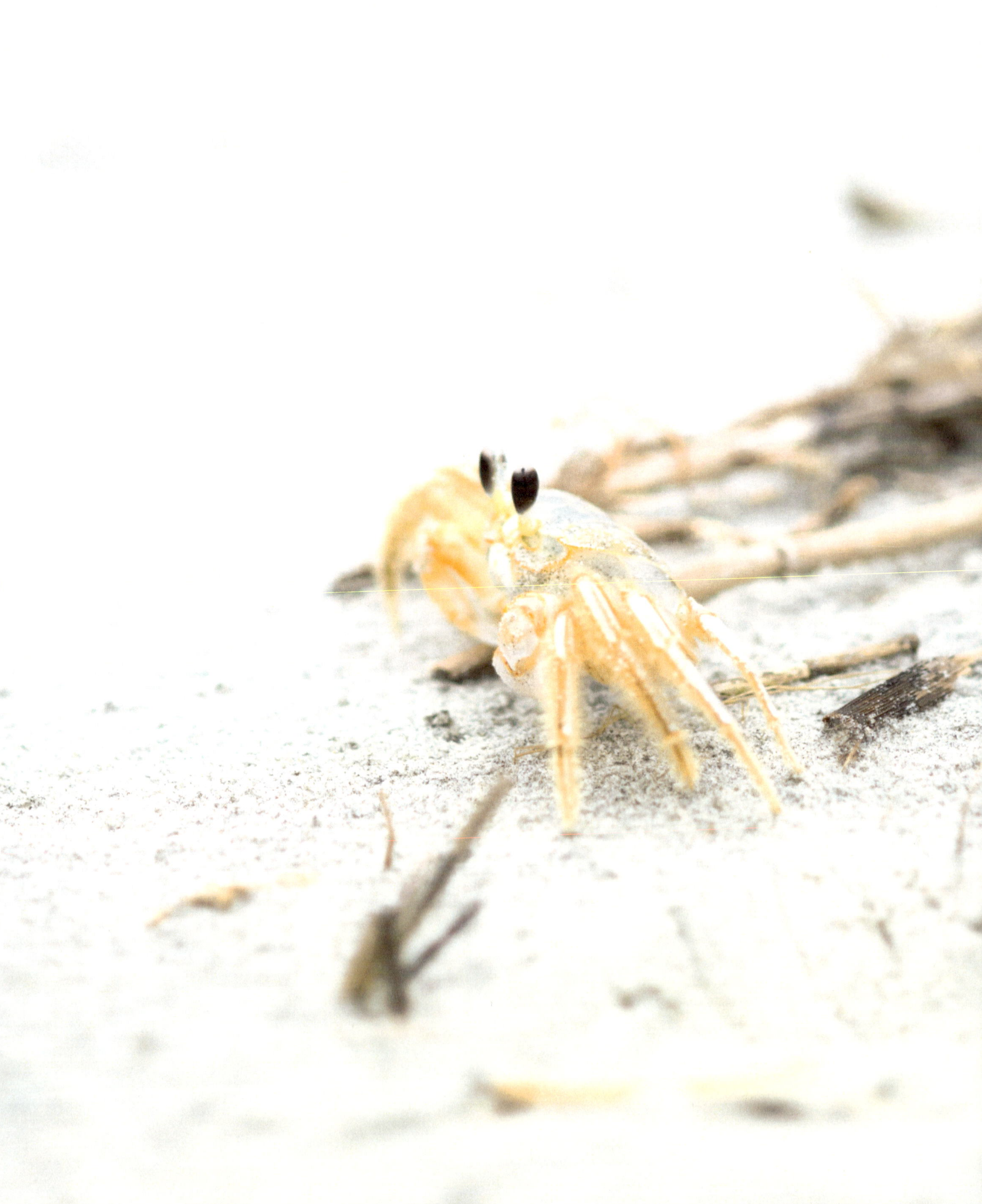

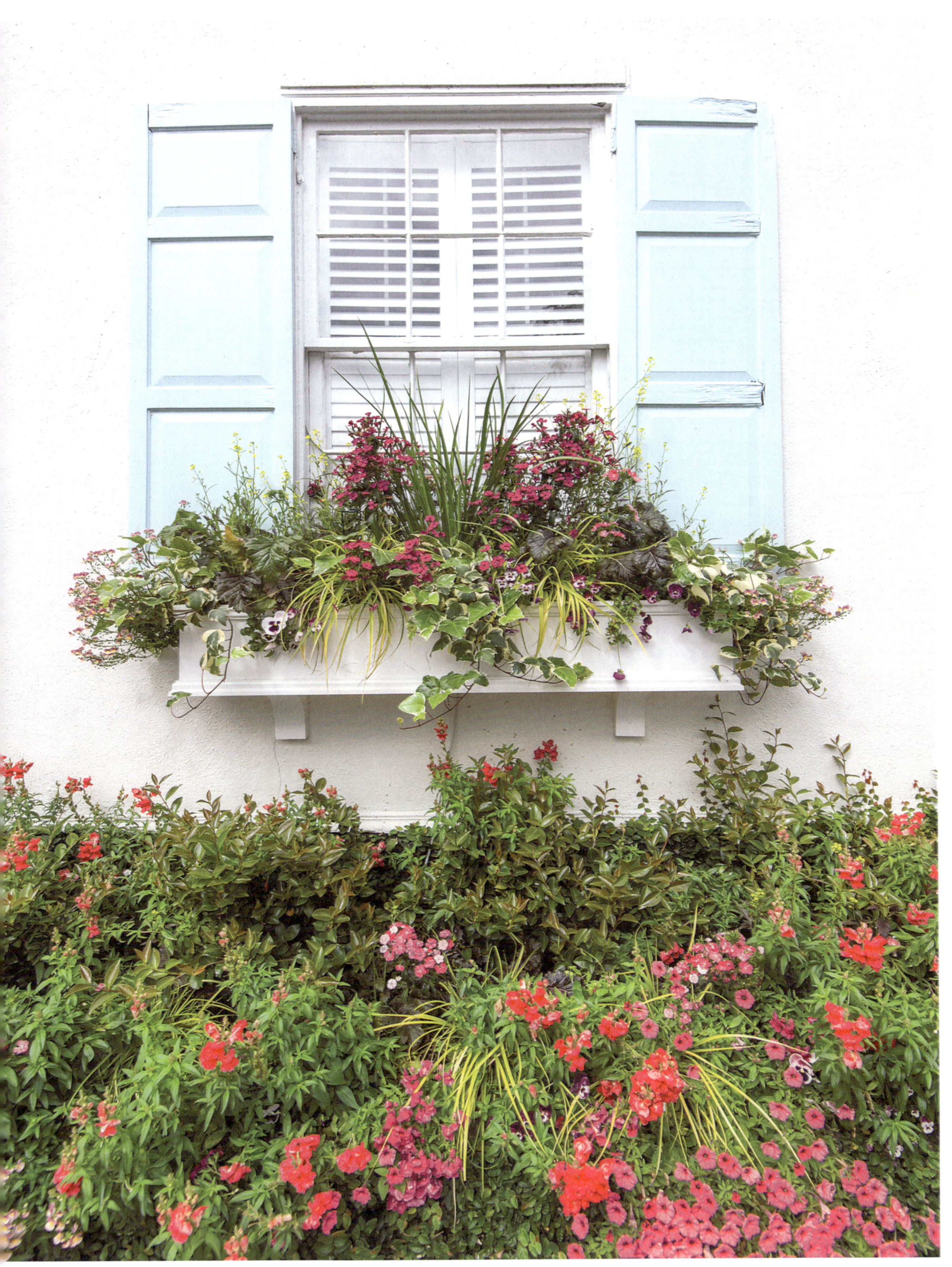

The Battery

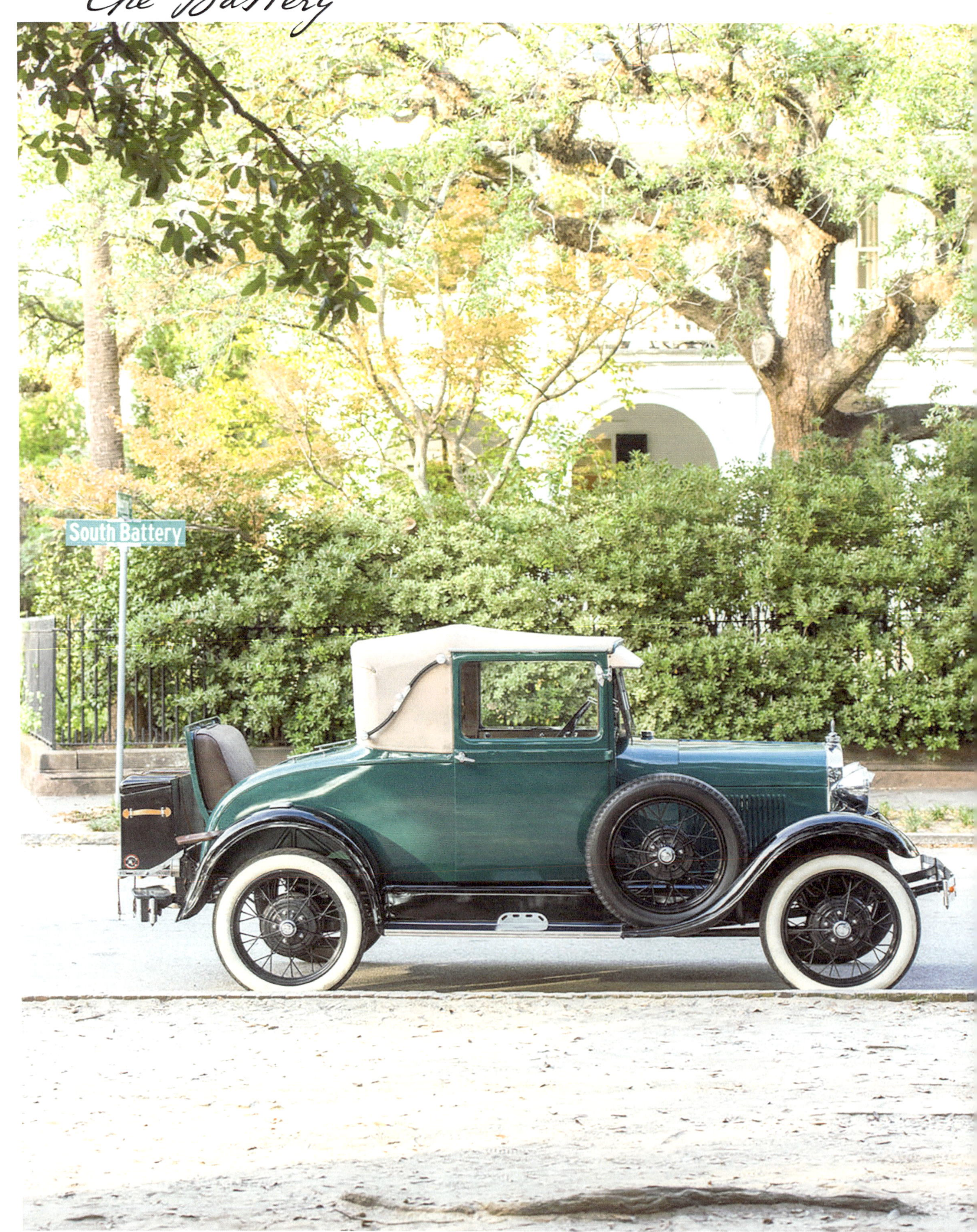

Stono River Park

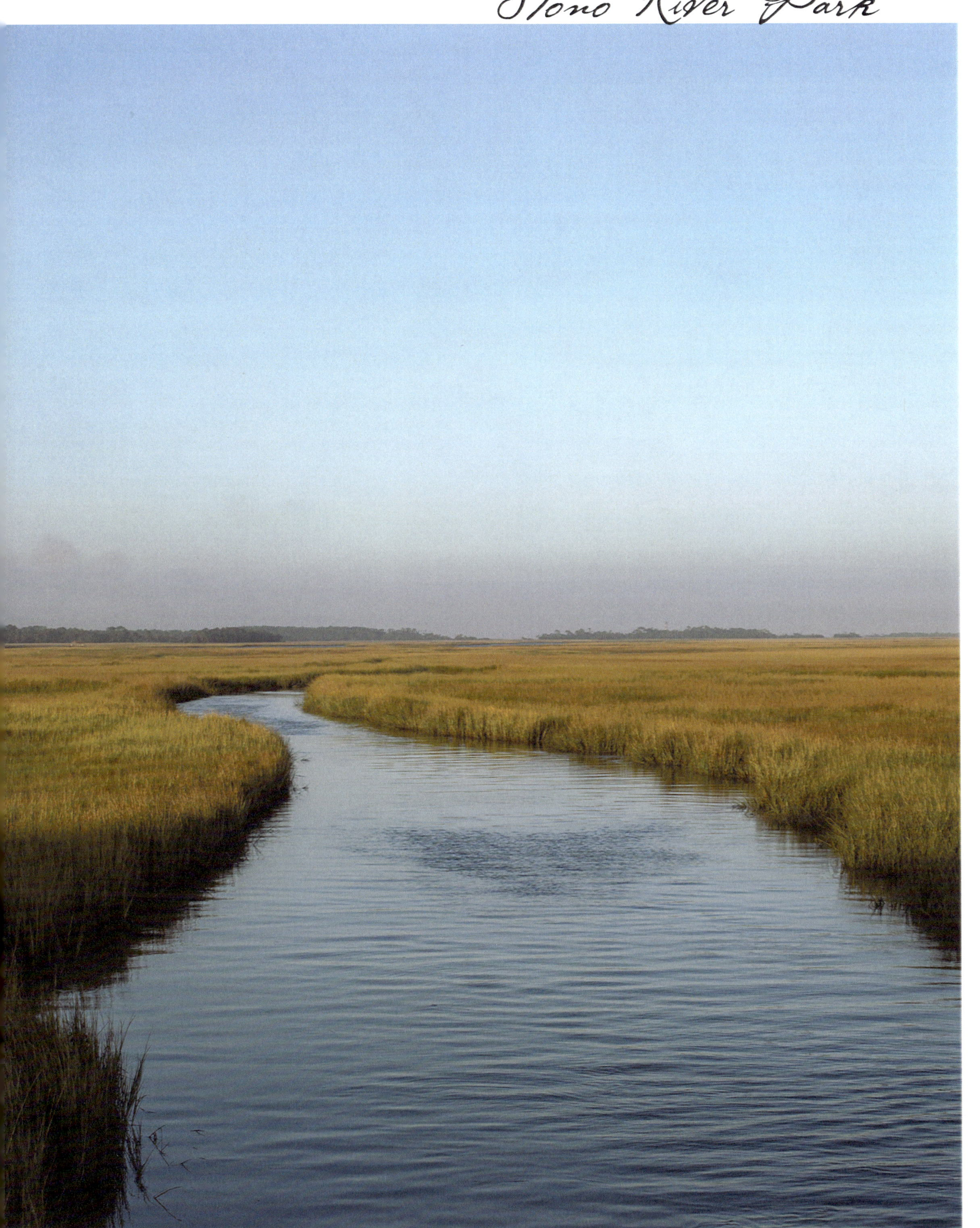

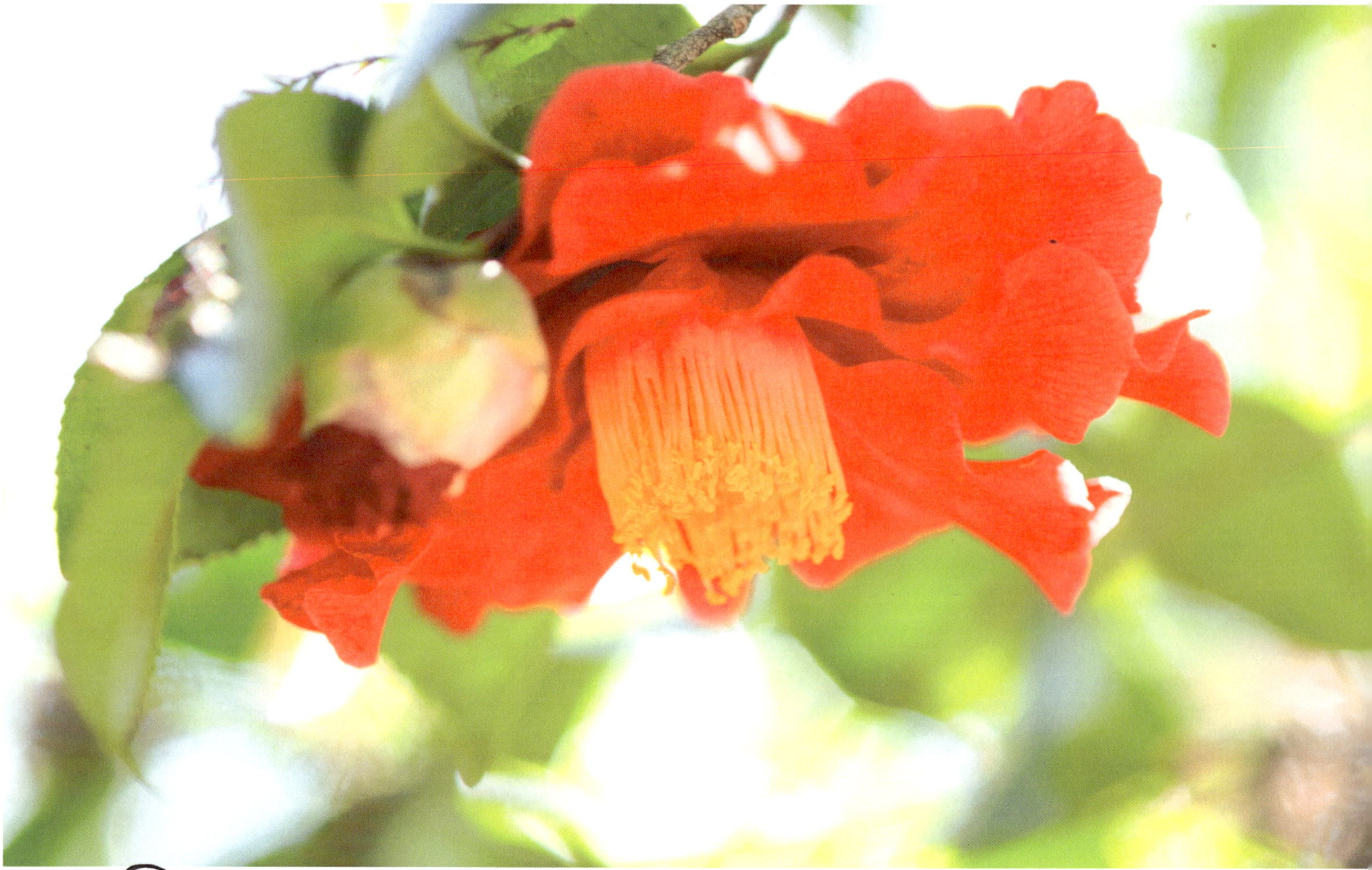

Magnolia Plantation & Gardens

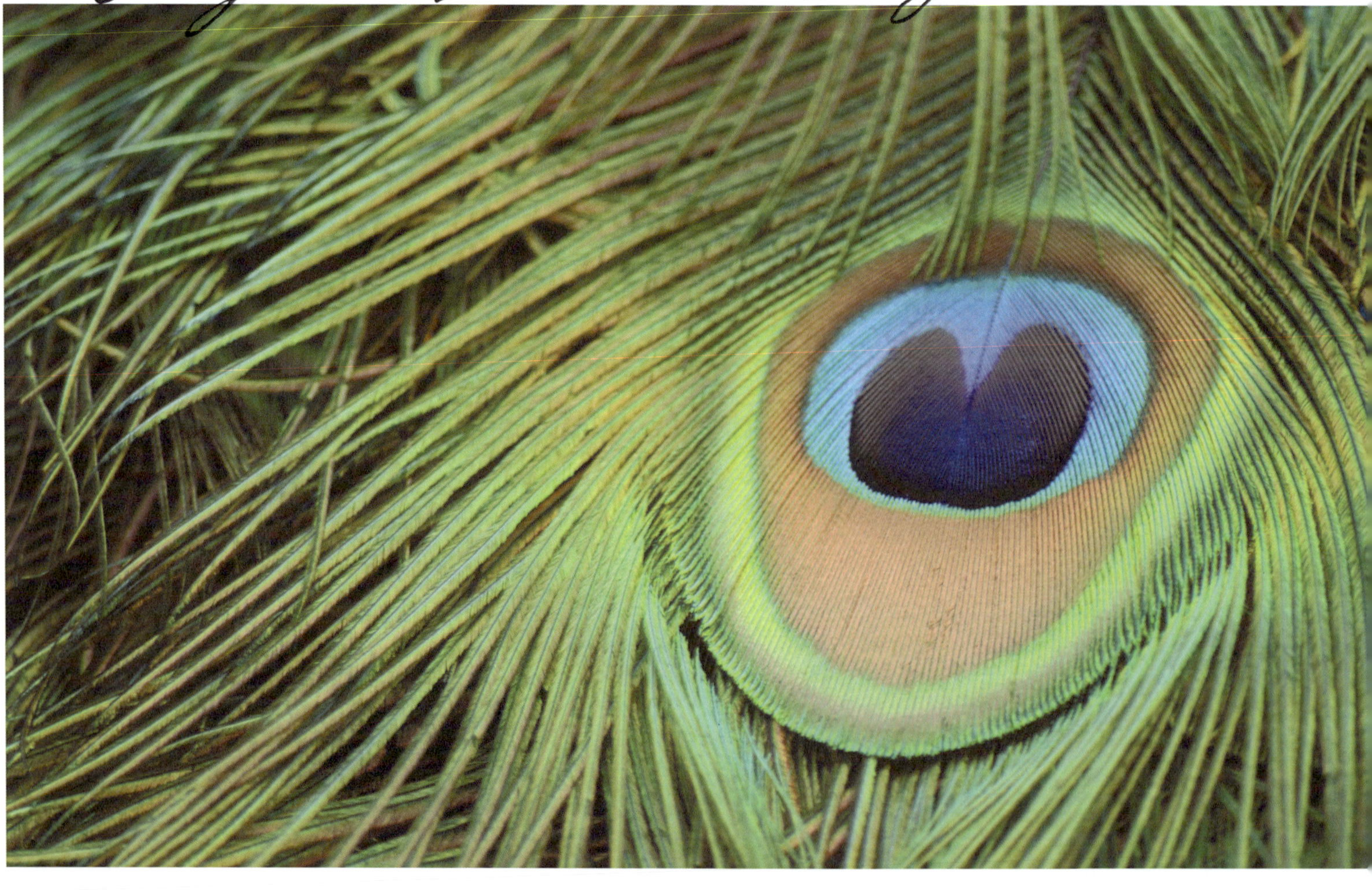

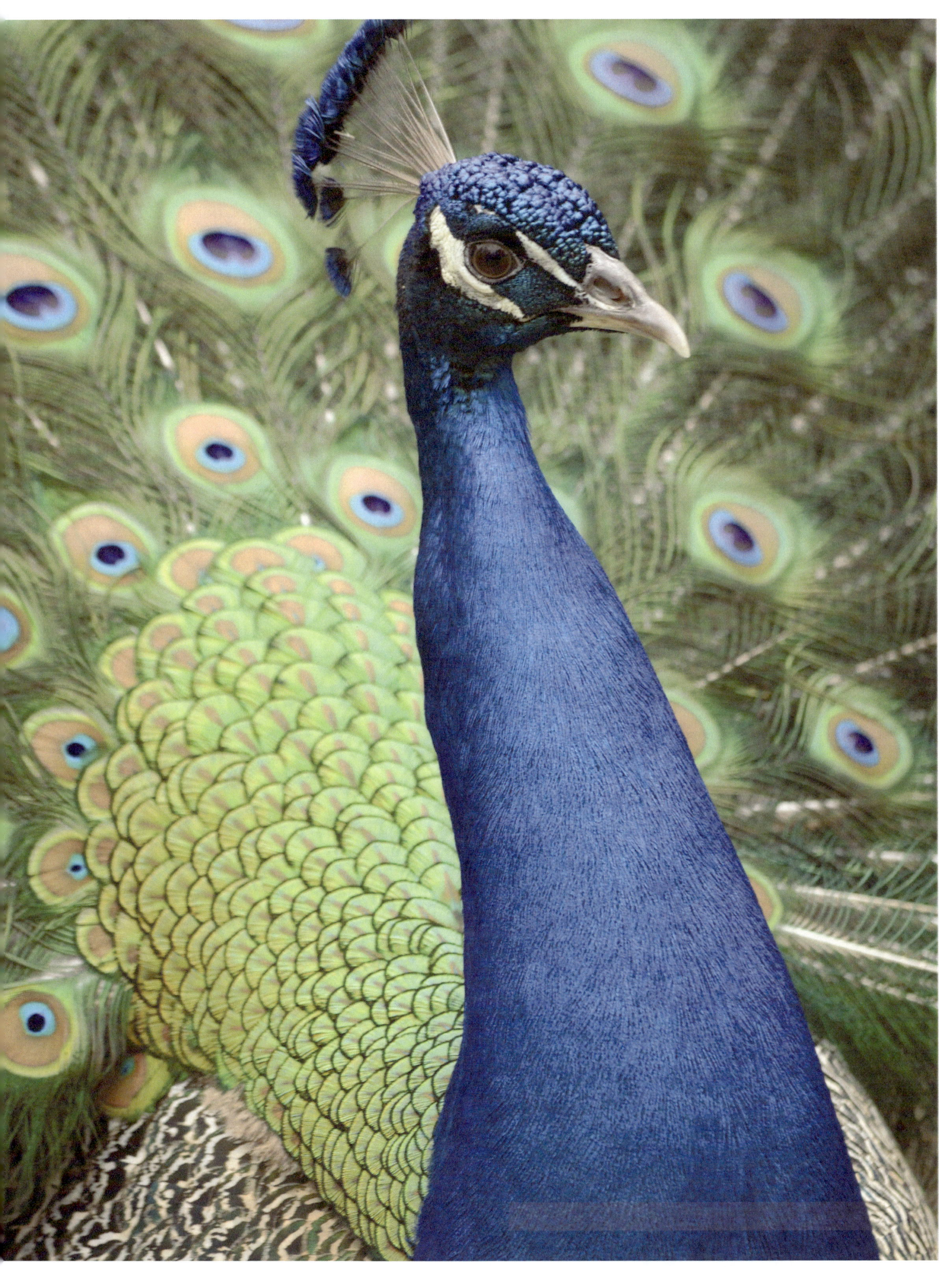

Rainbow Row

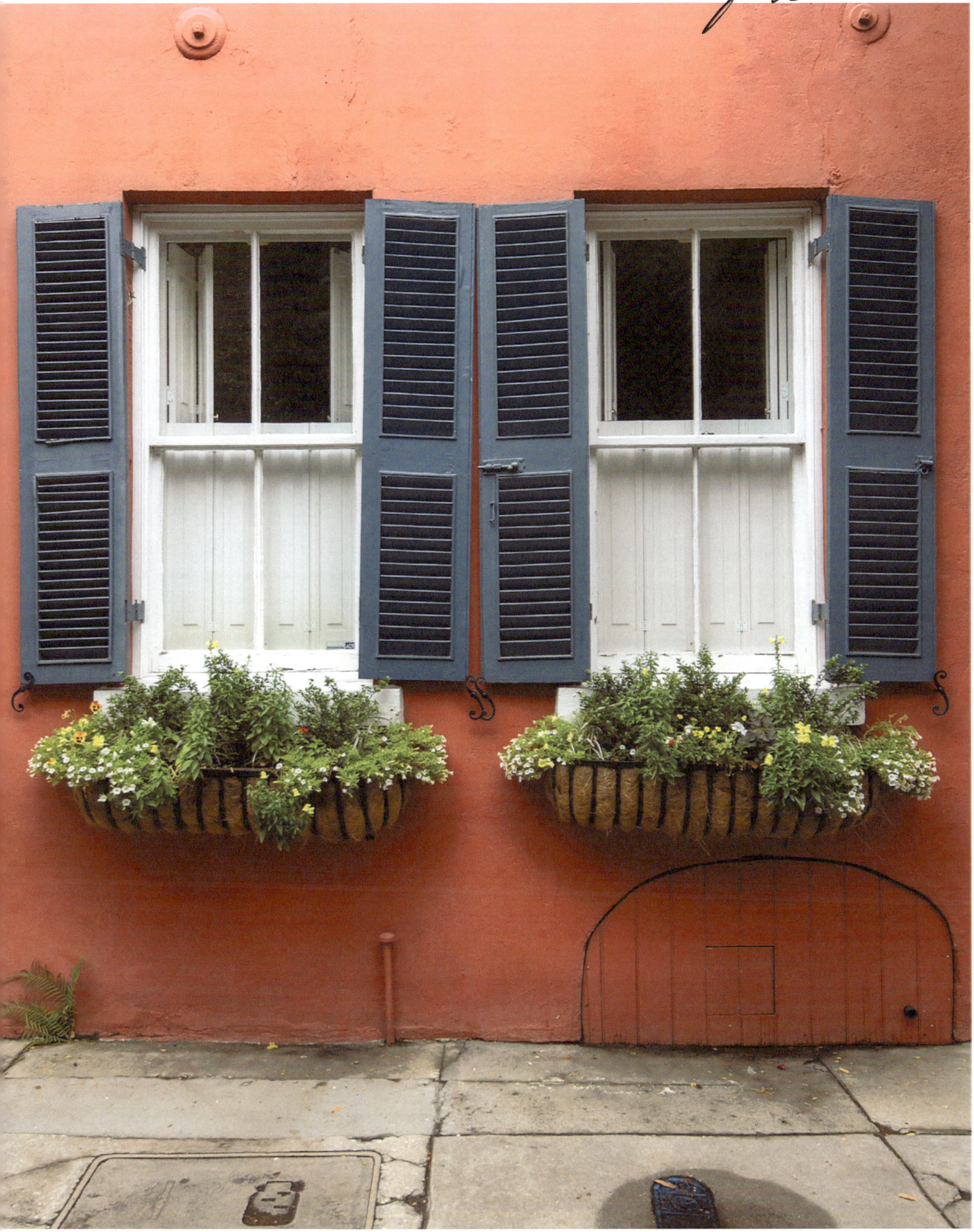

South of Broad

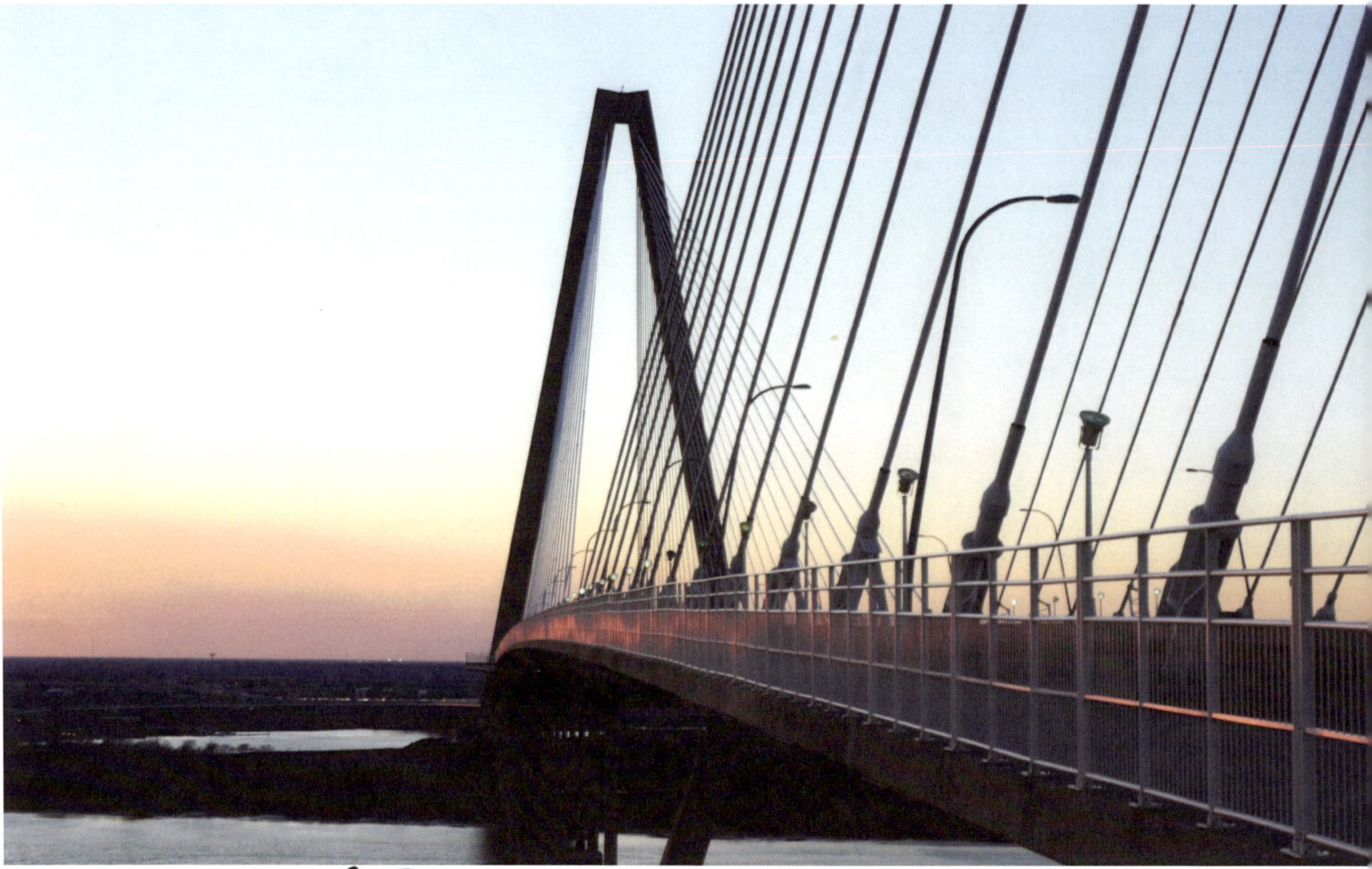

Ravenel Bridge

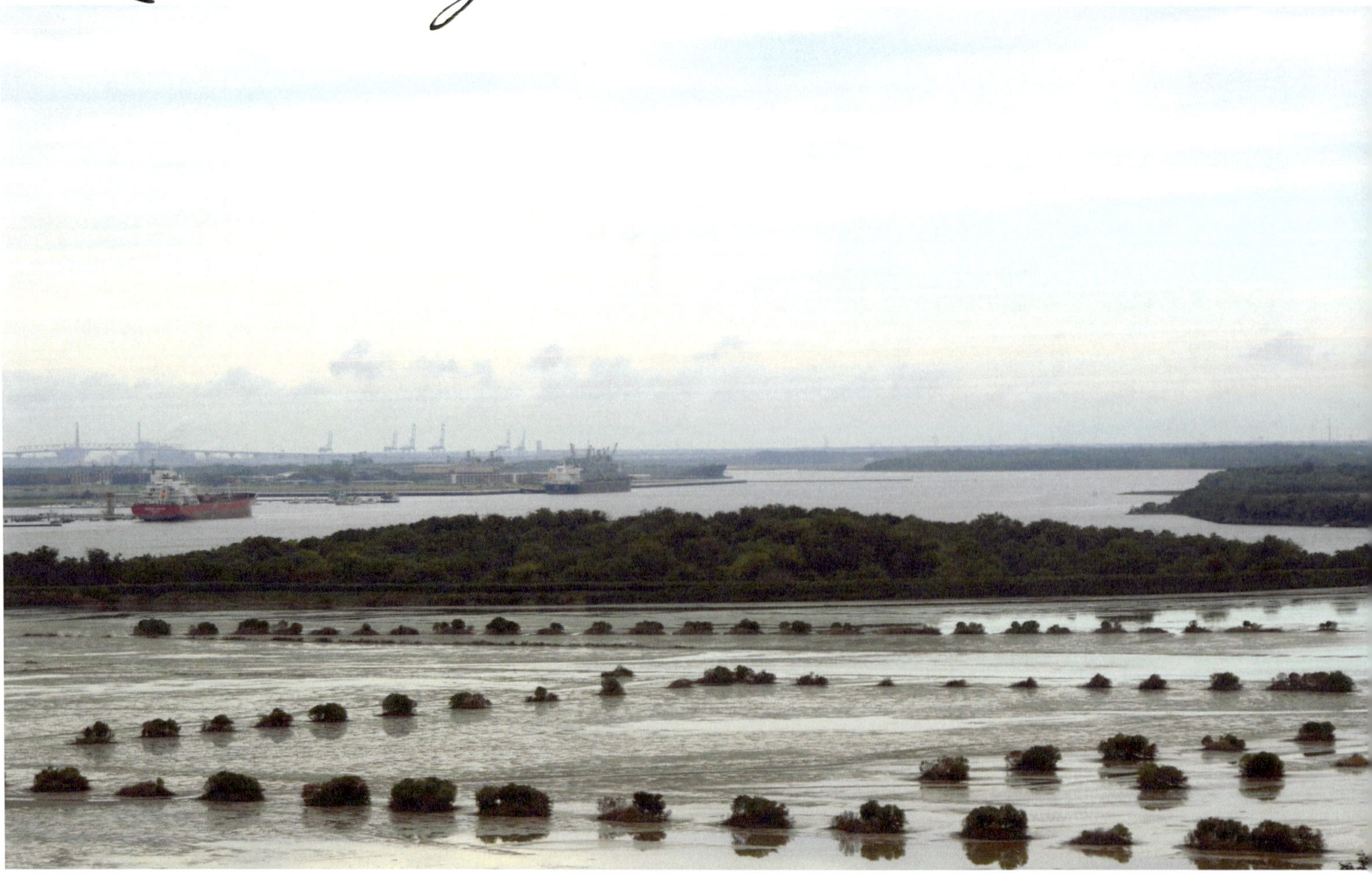

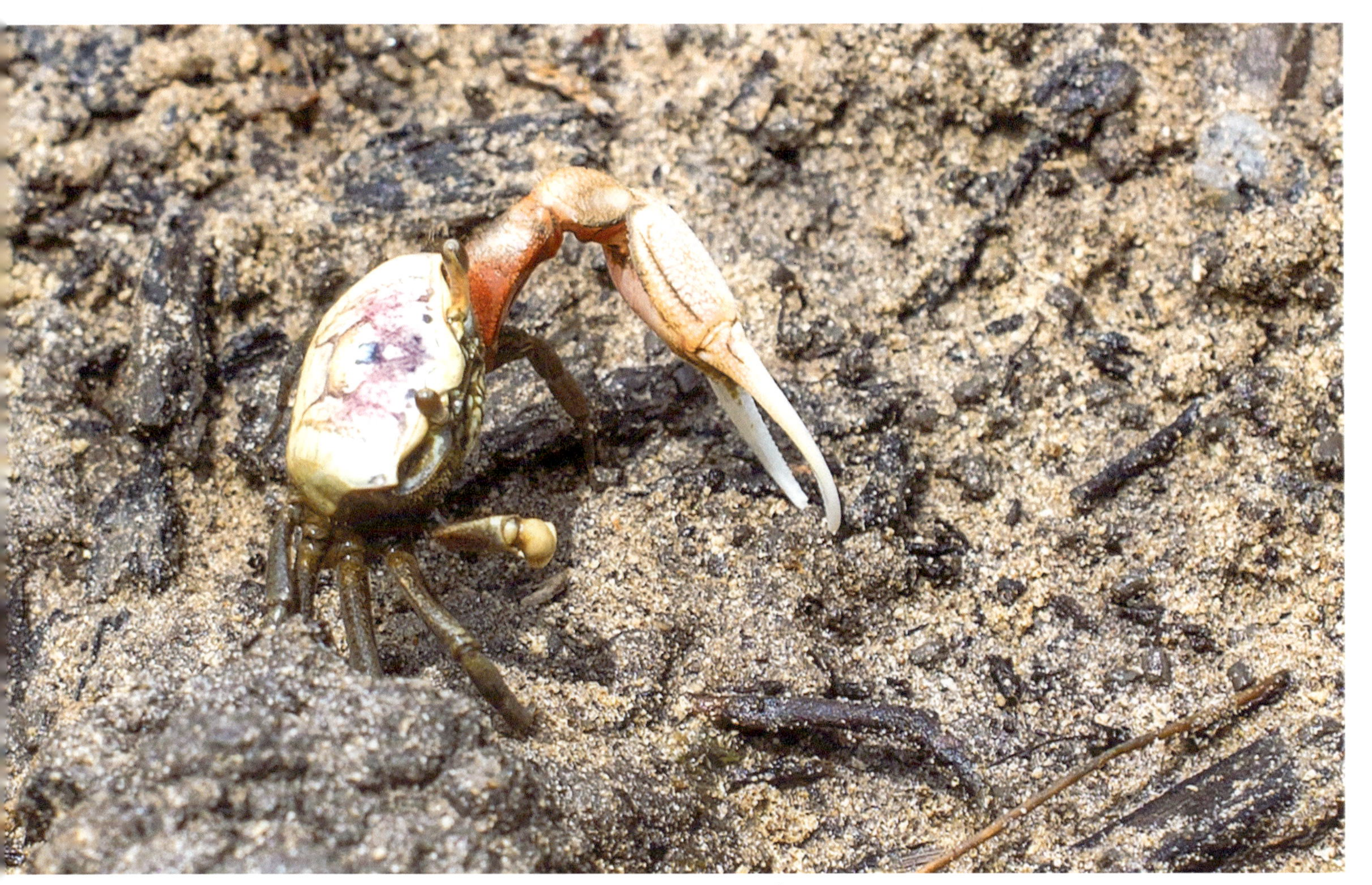

Stono River Park

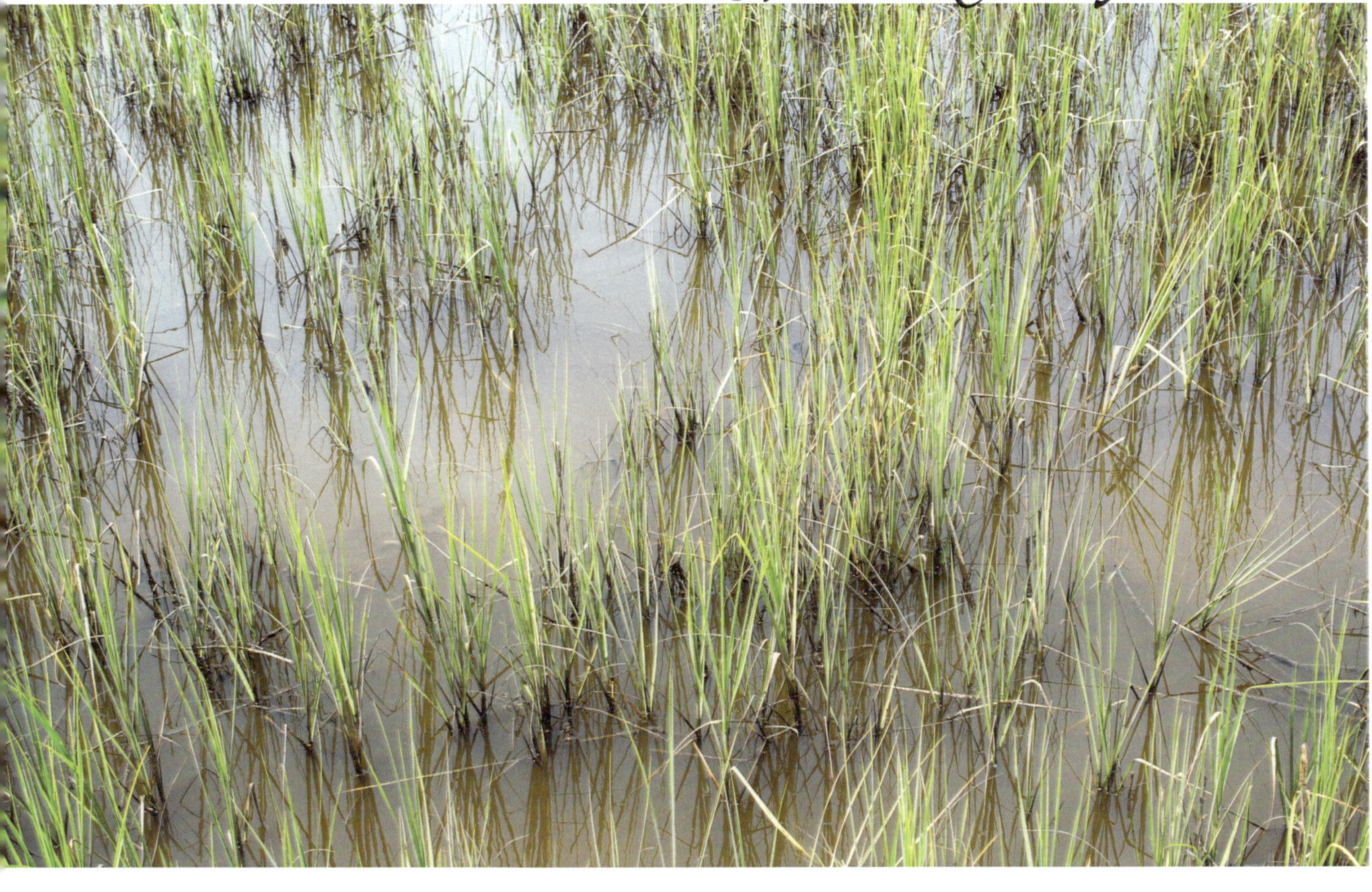

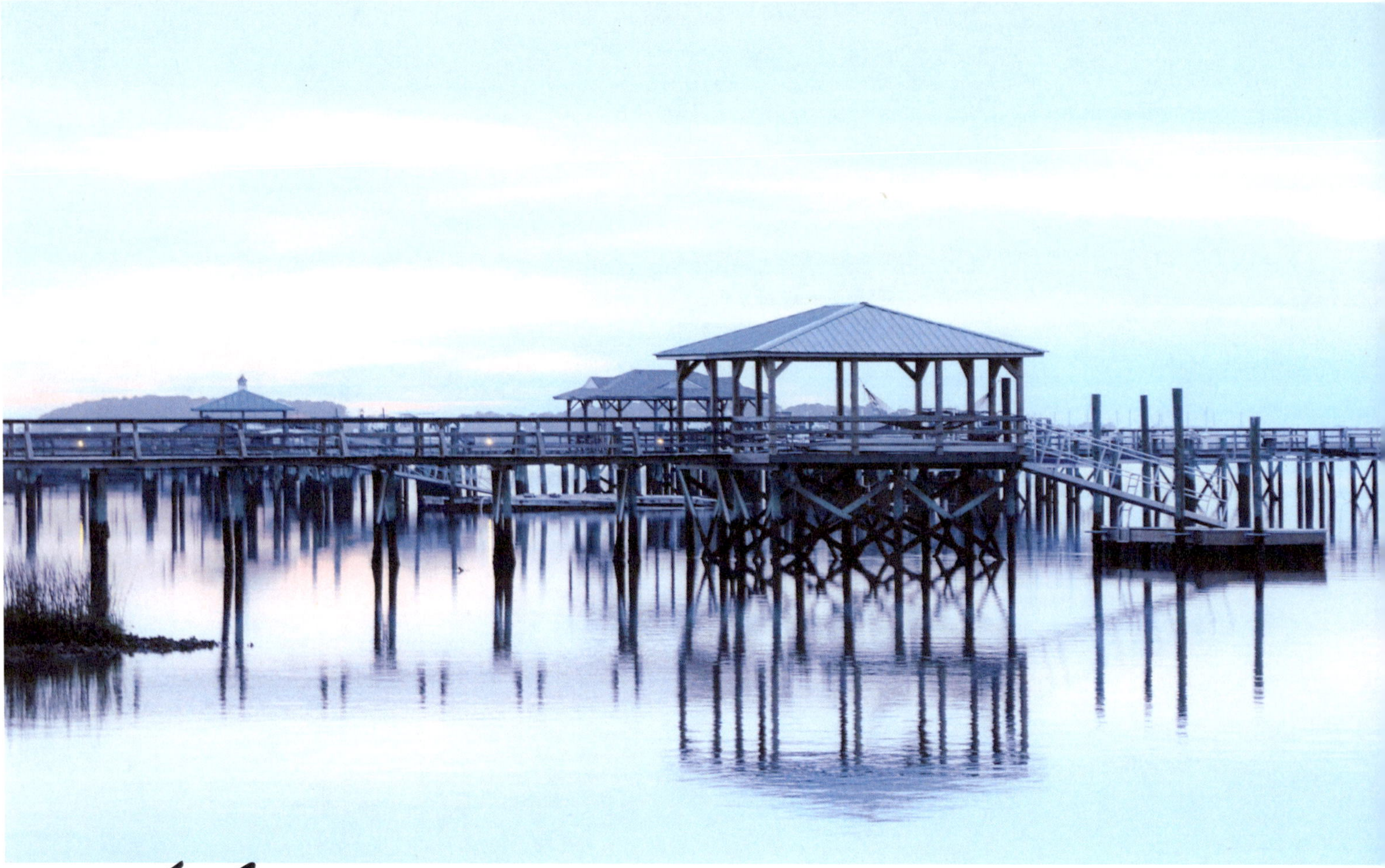

Folly Beach

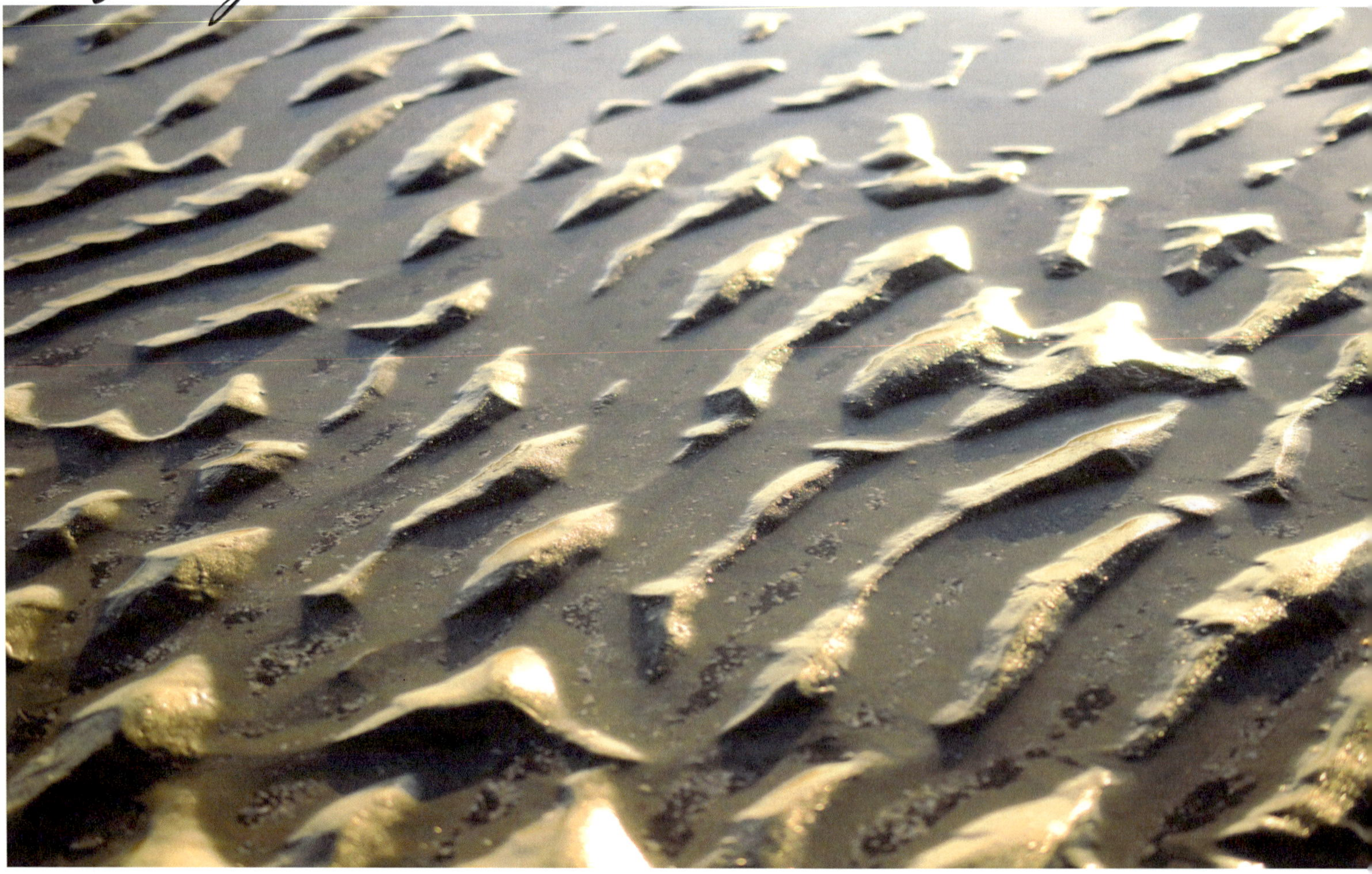

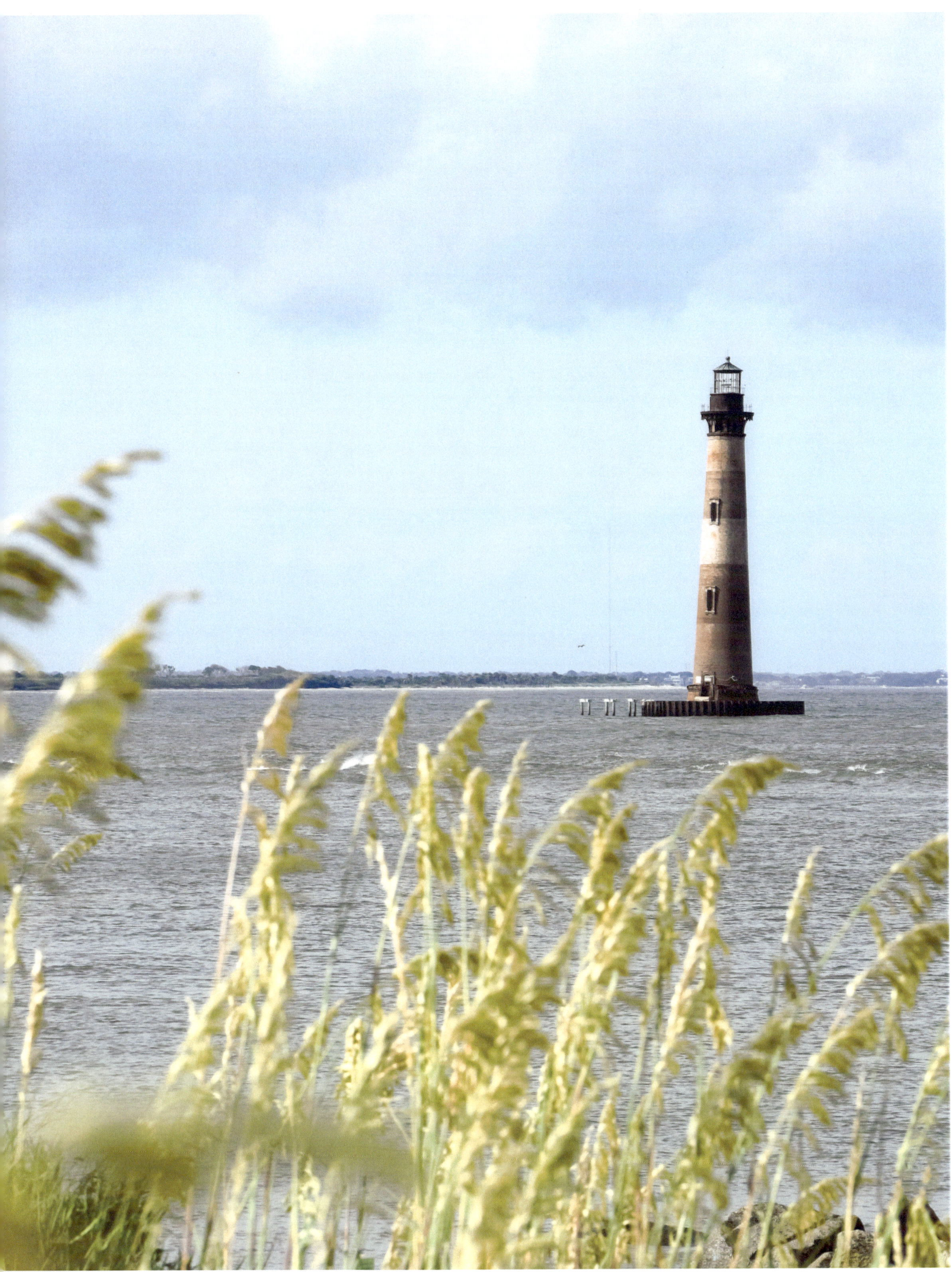

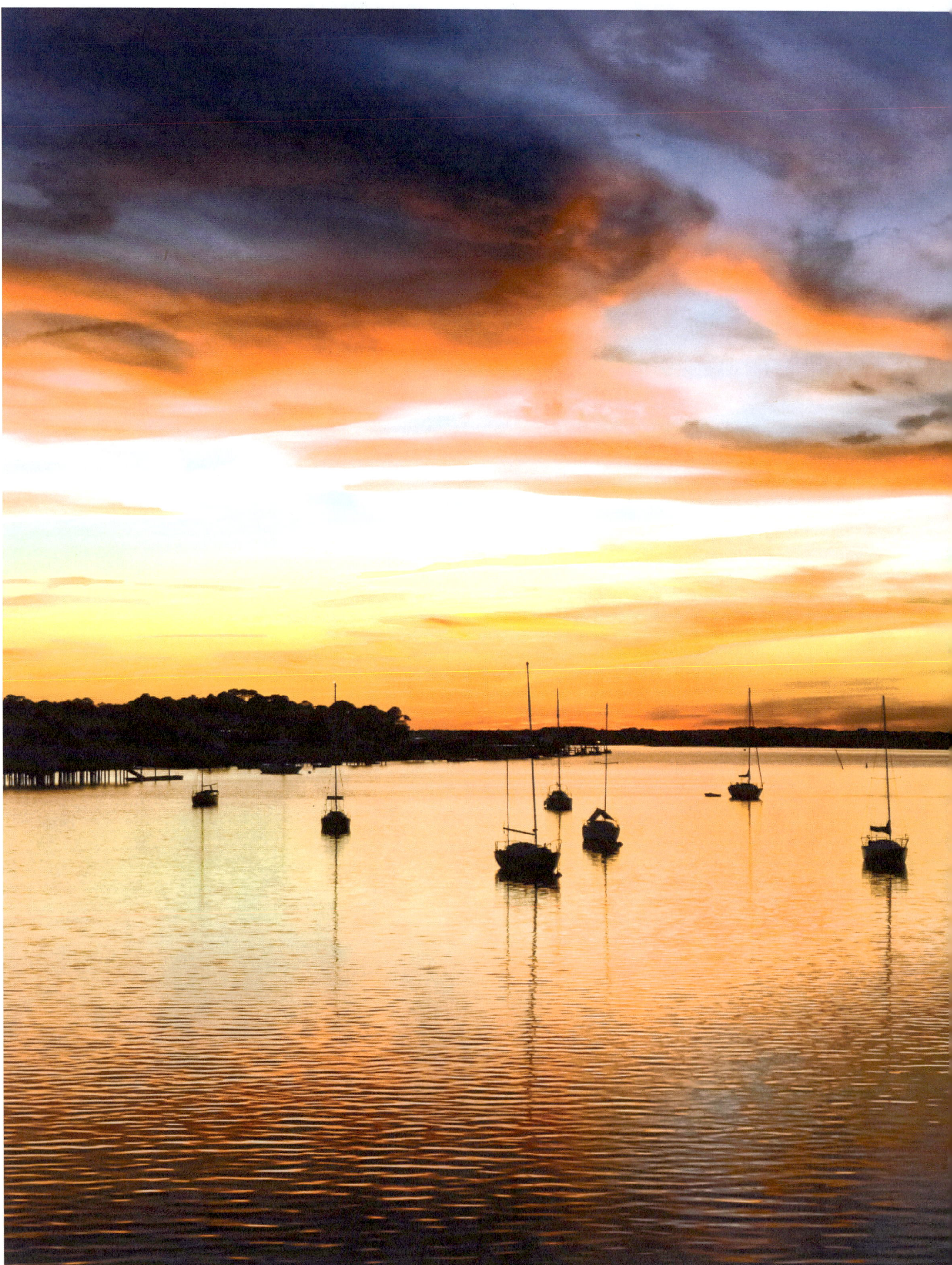

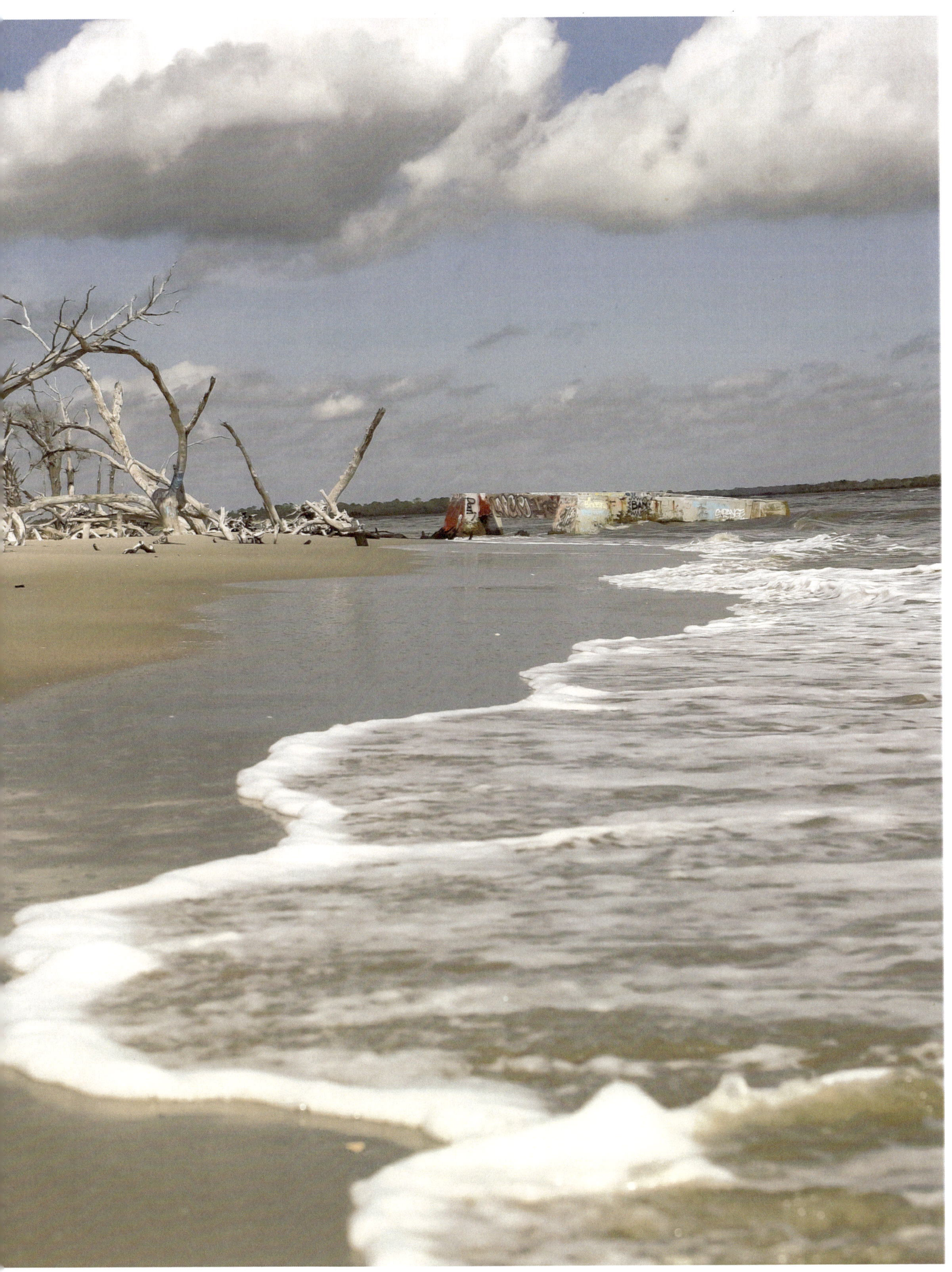

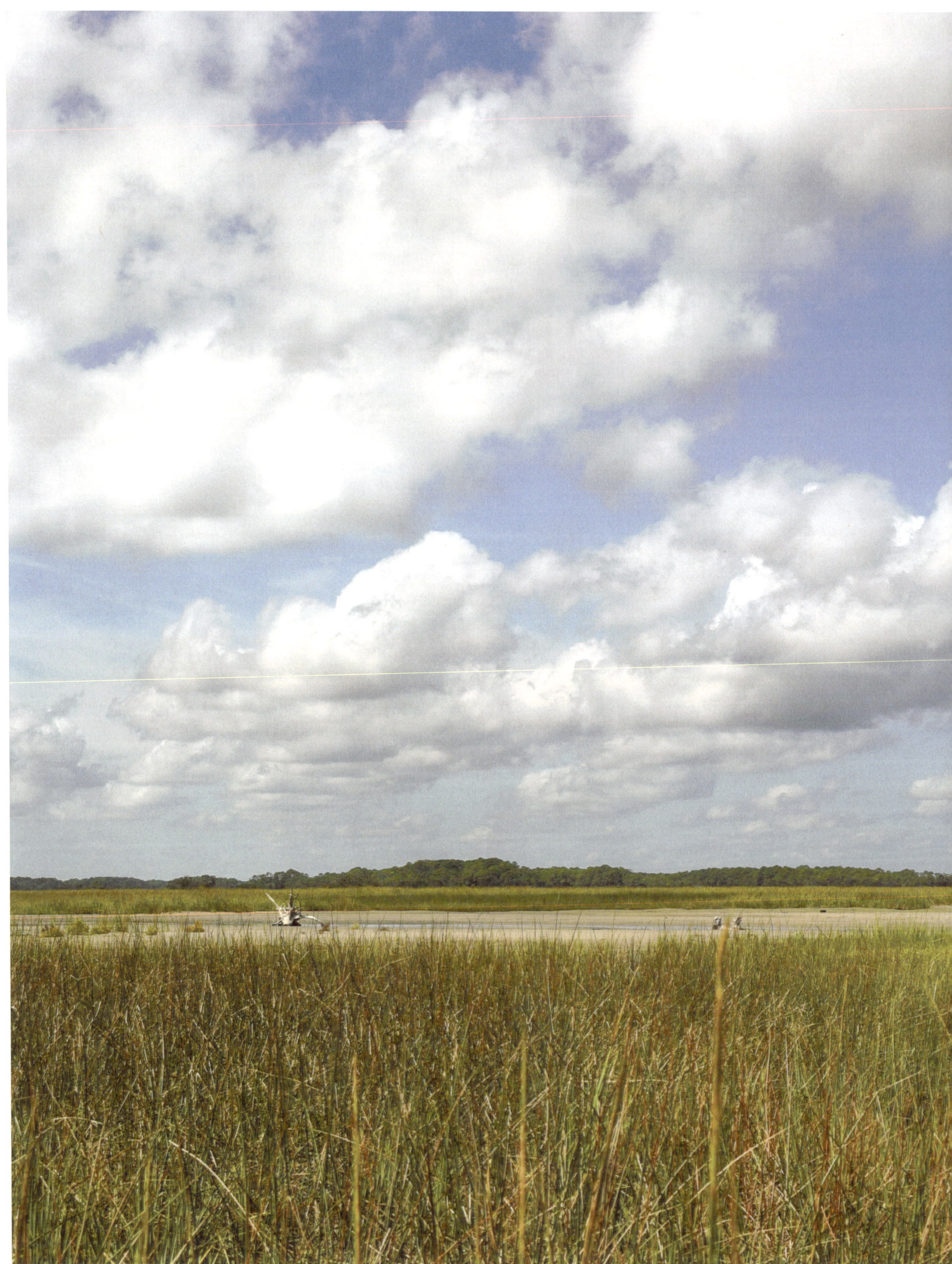

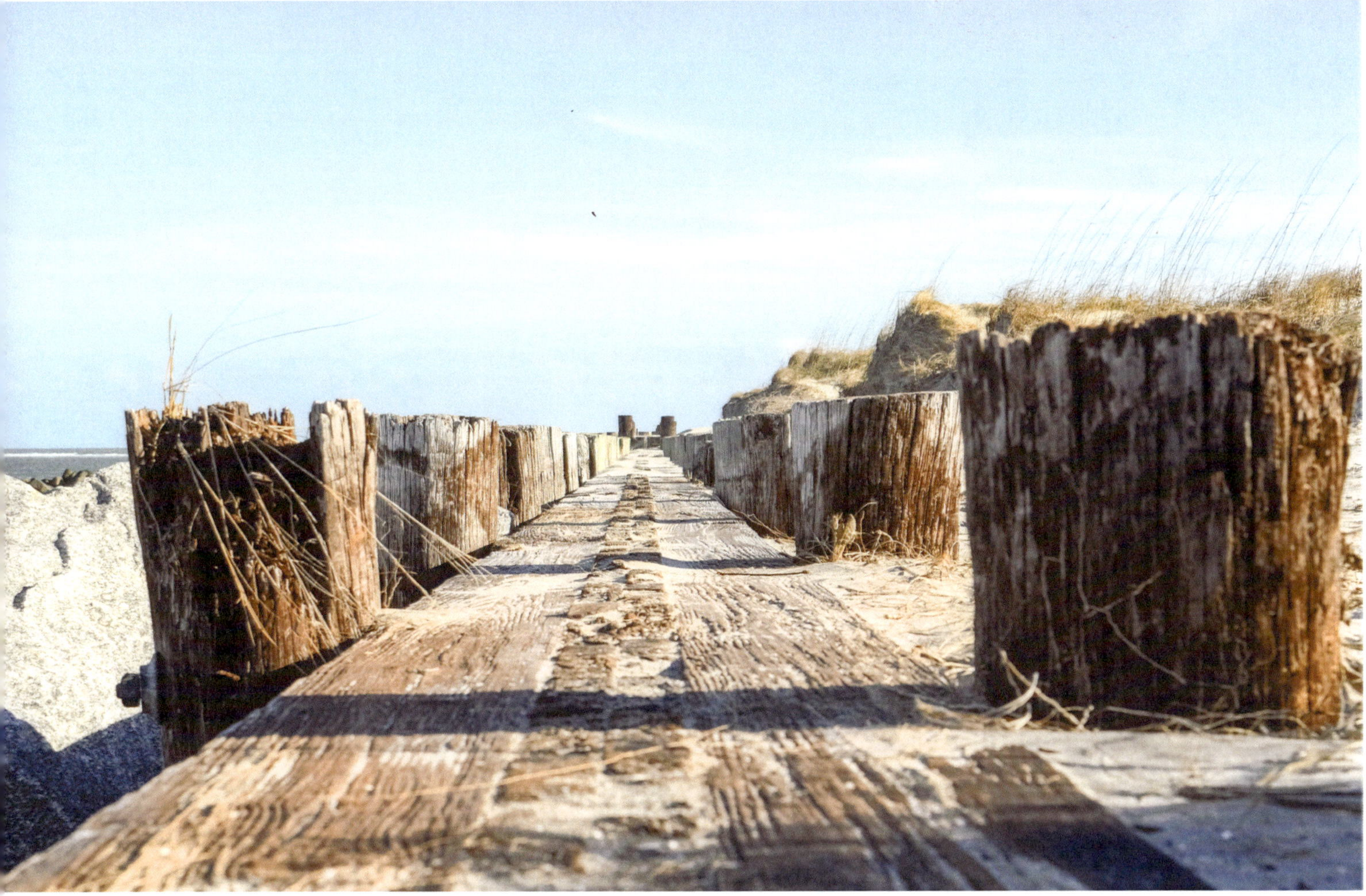

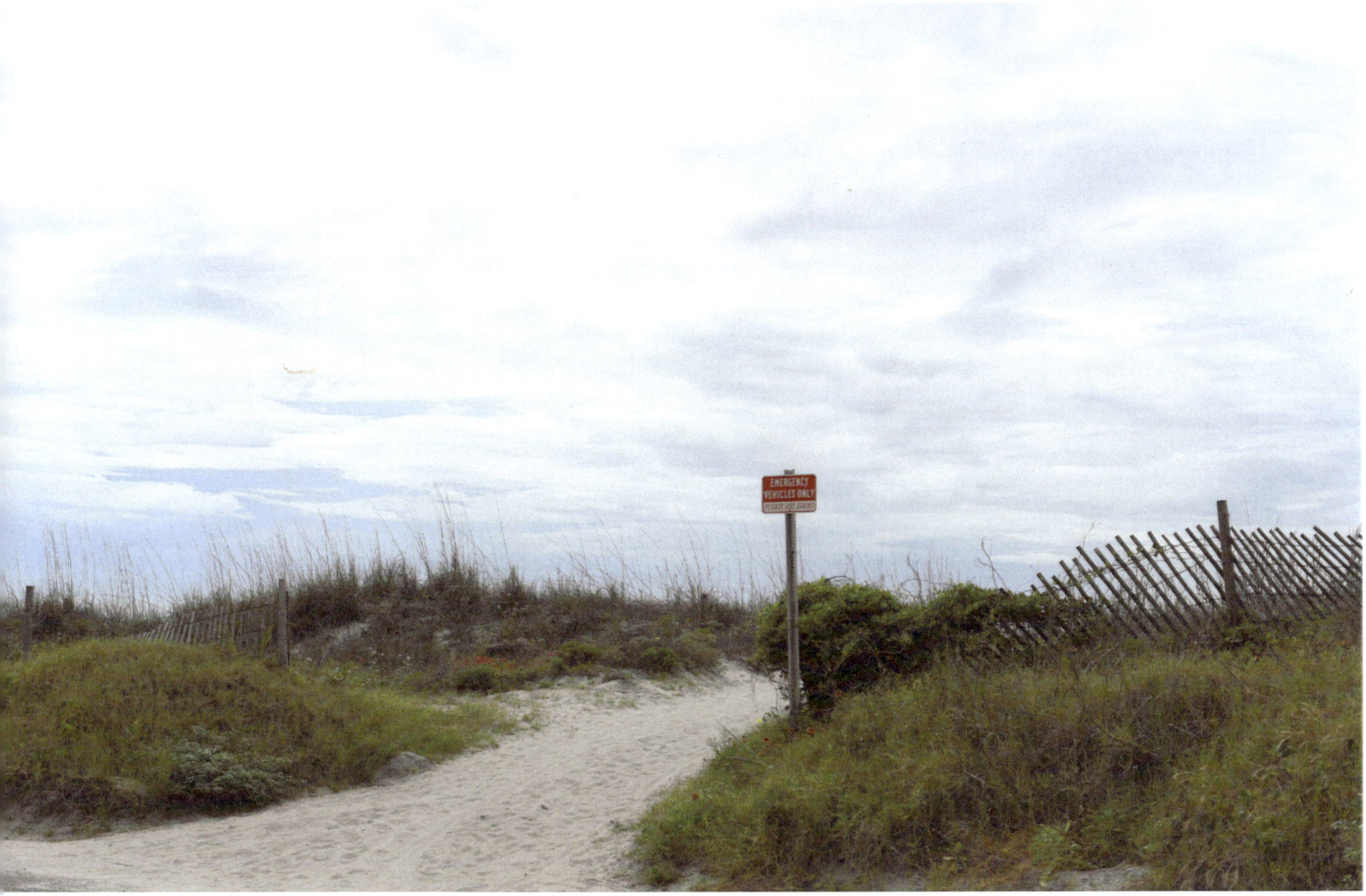

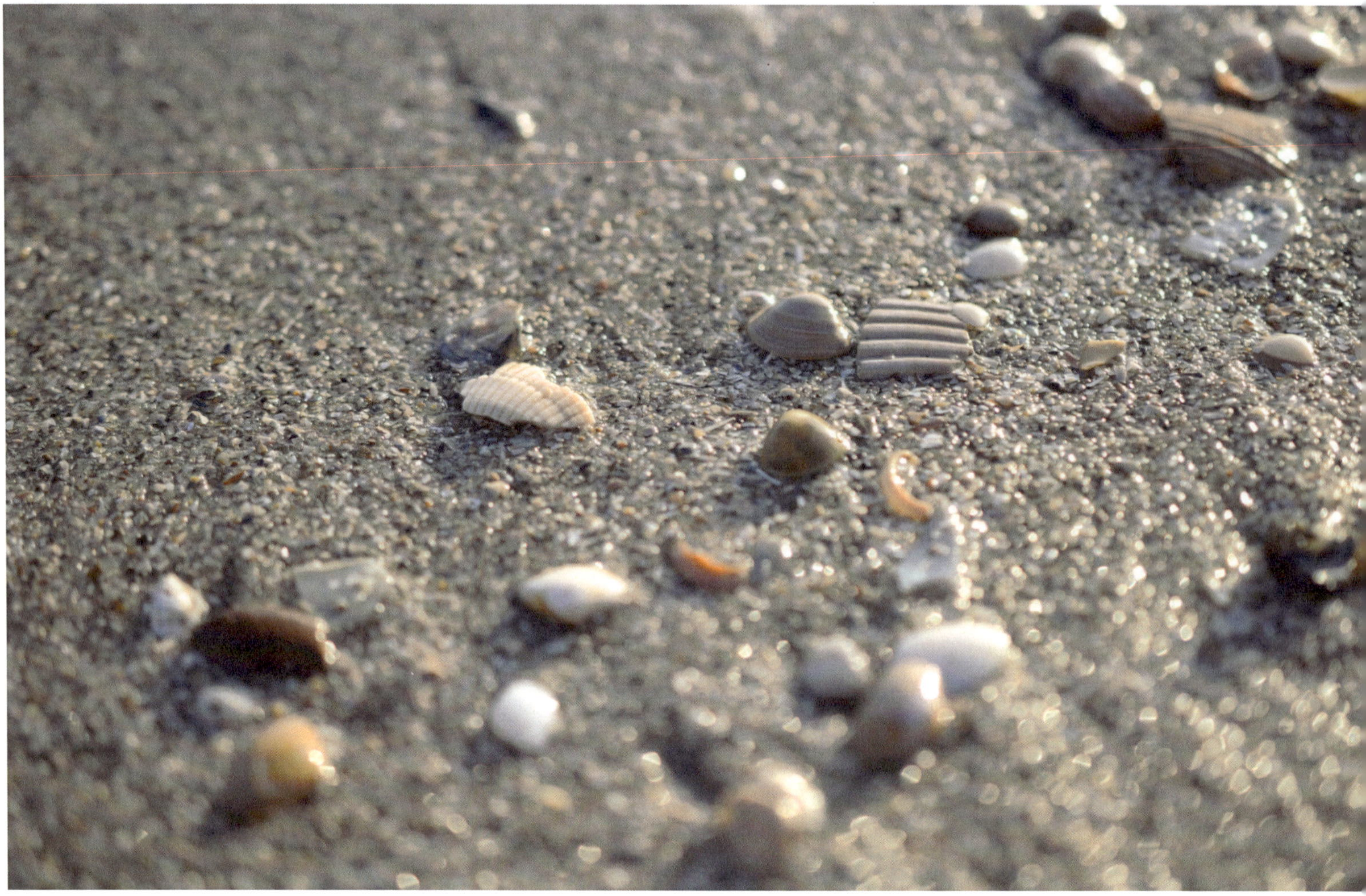

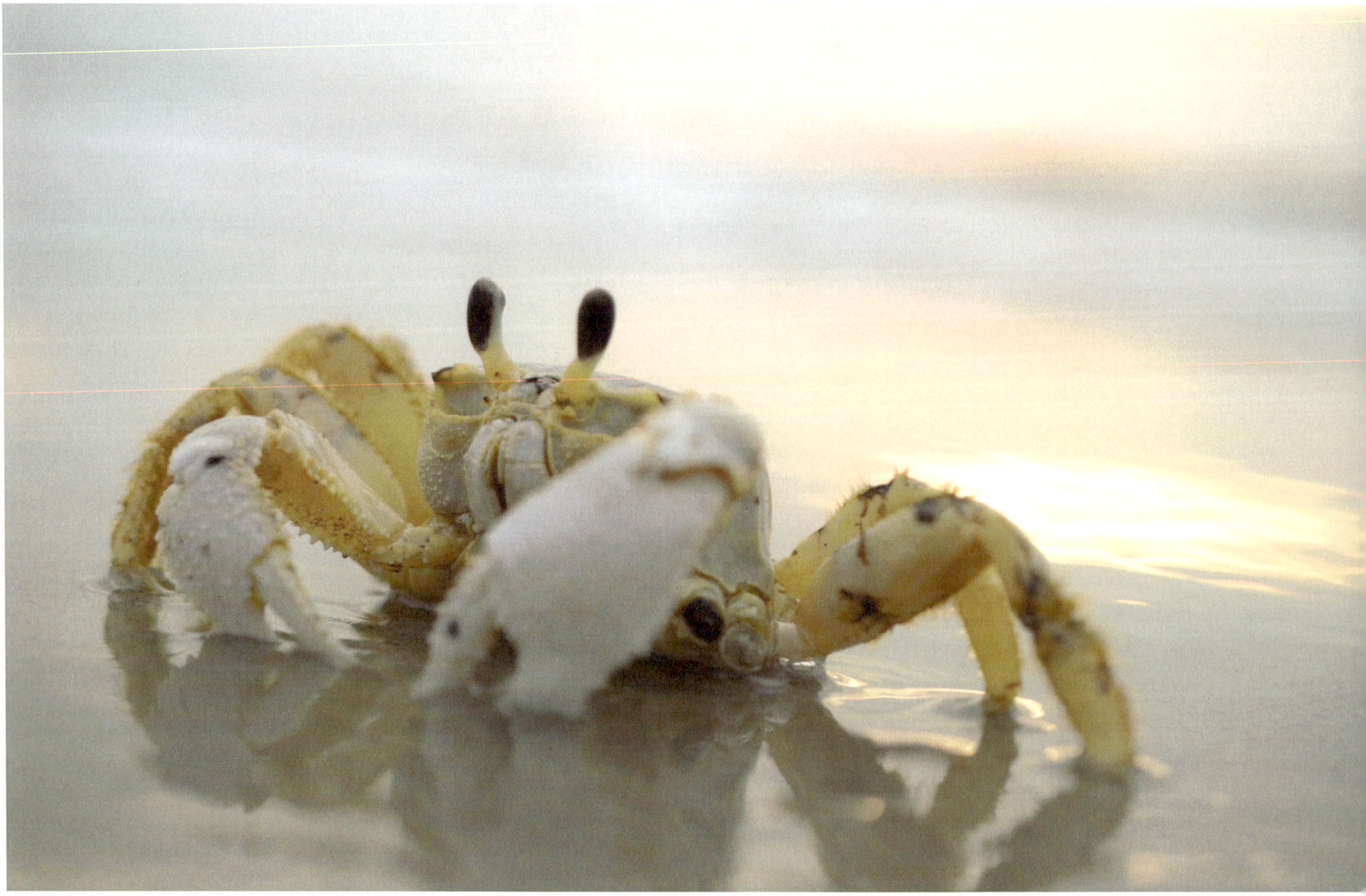

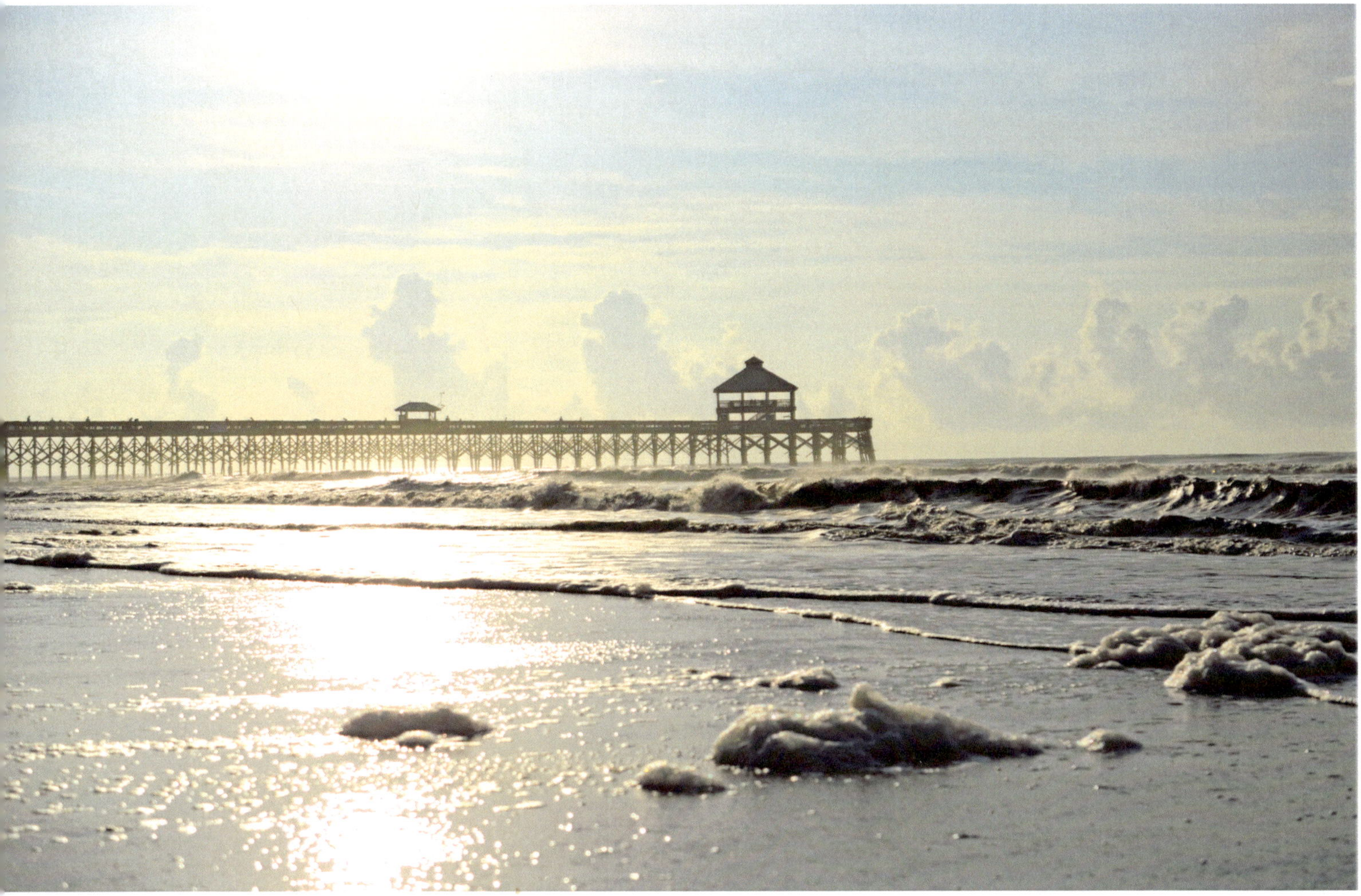

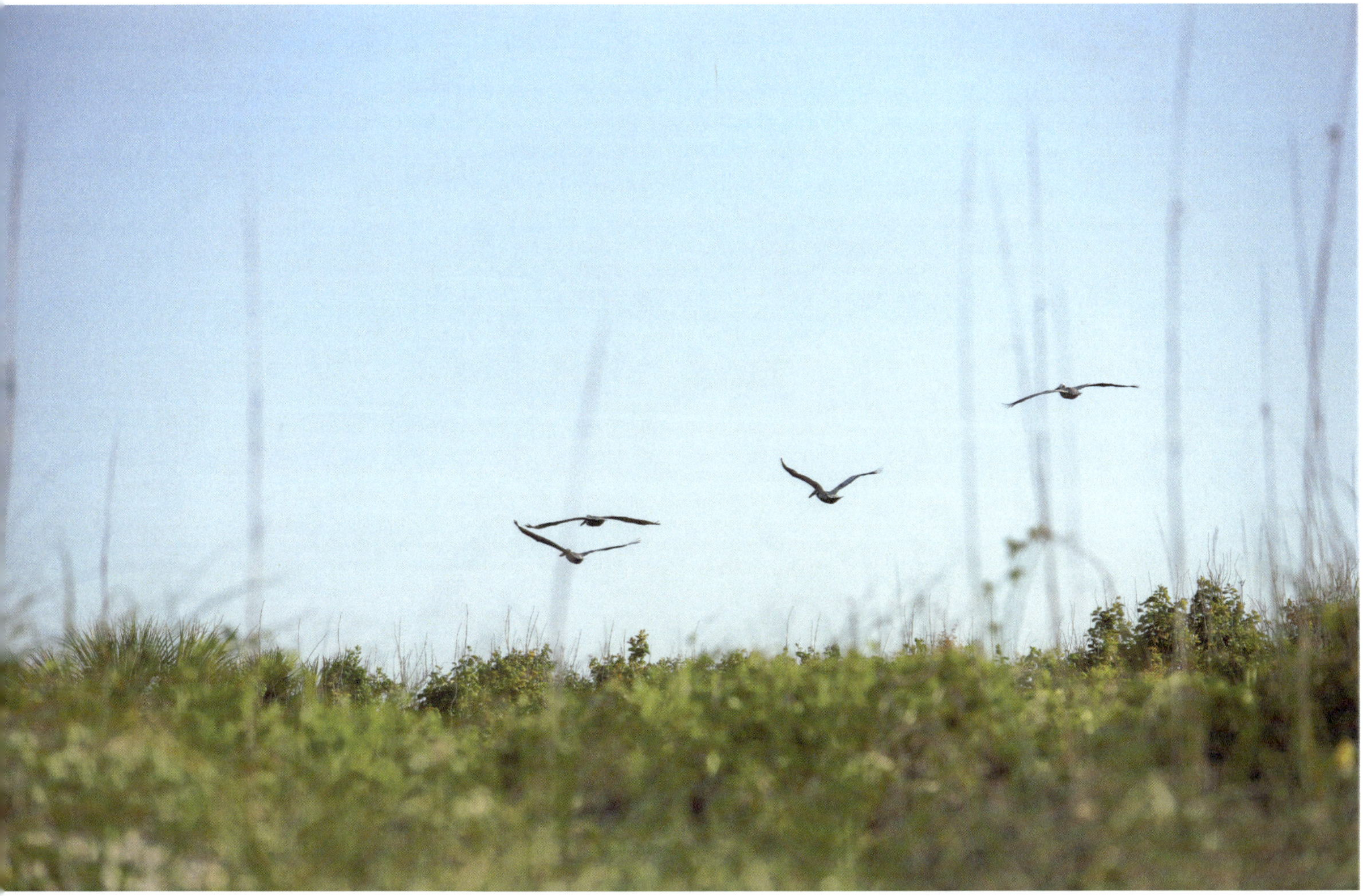

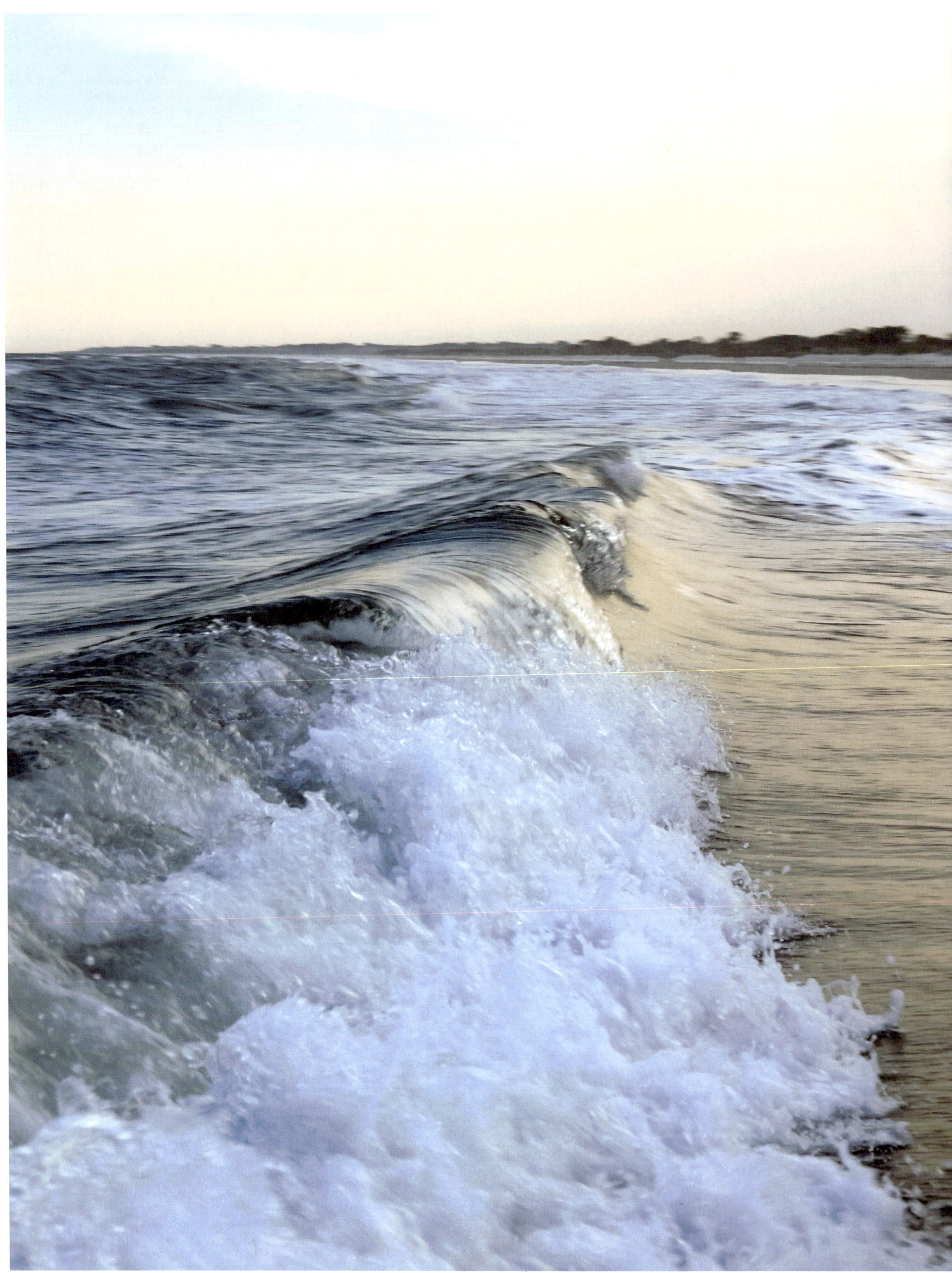

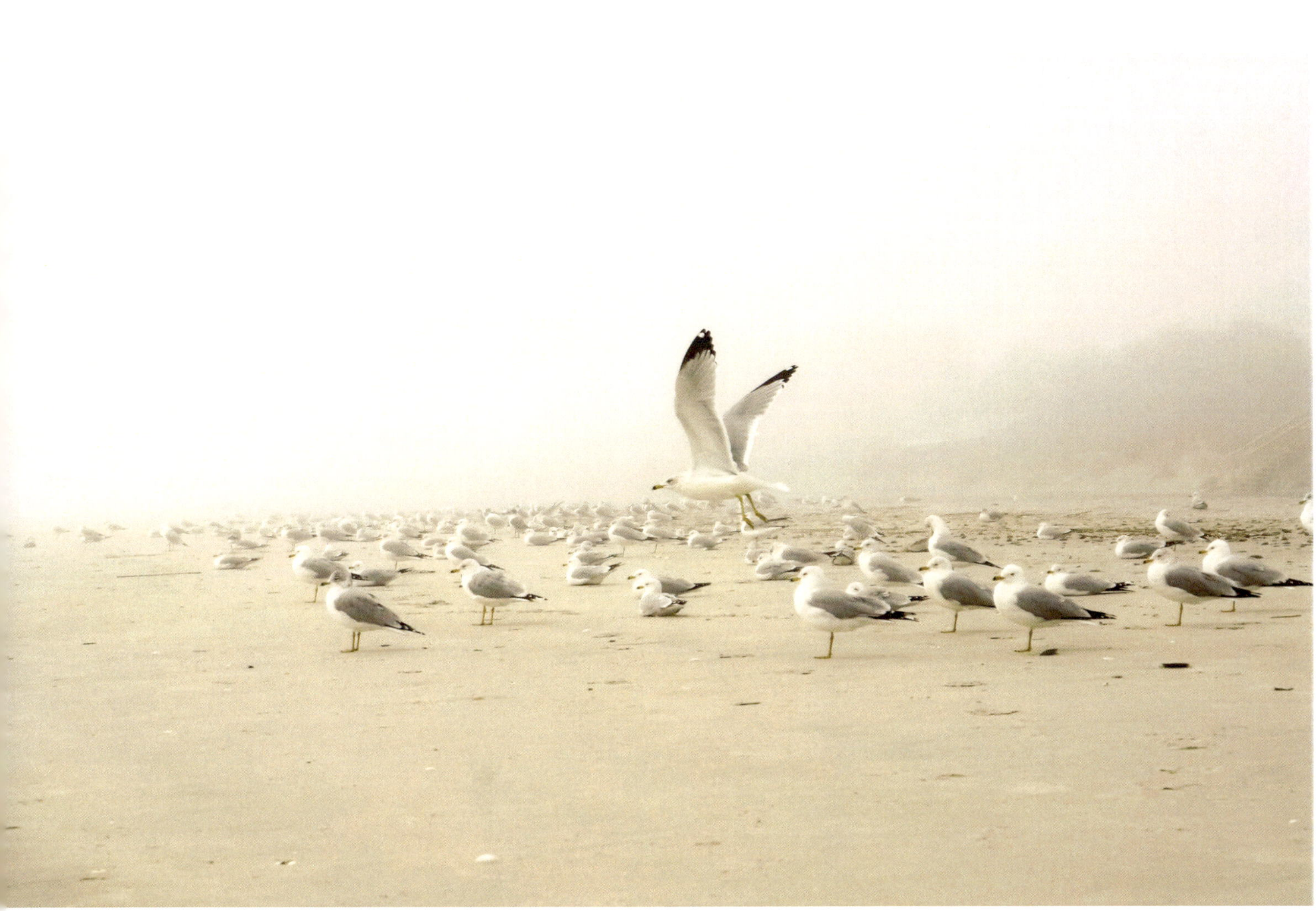

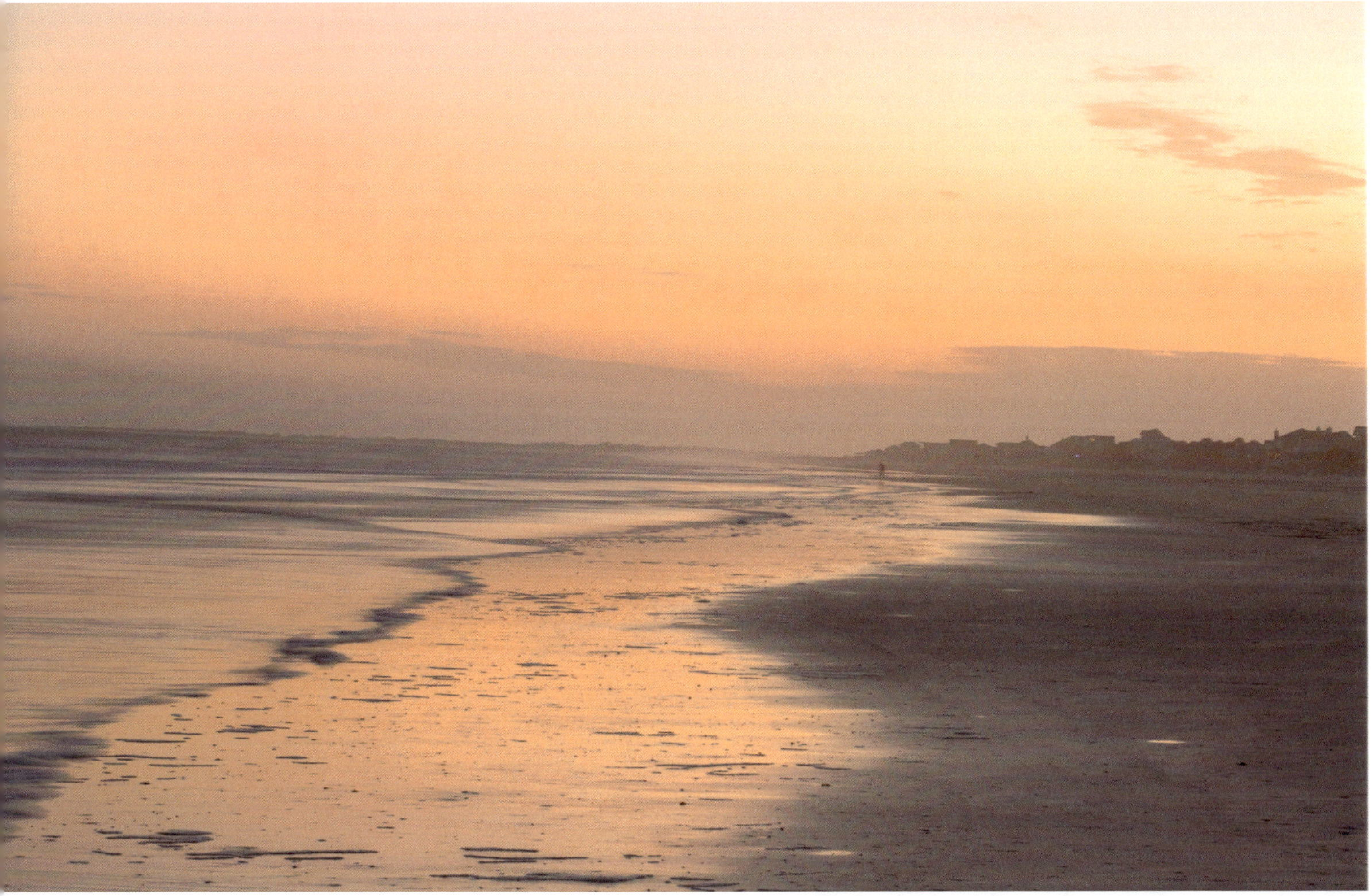

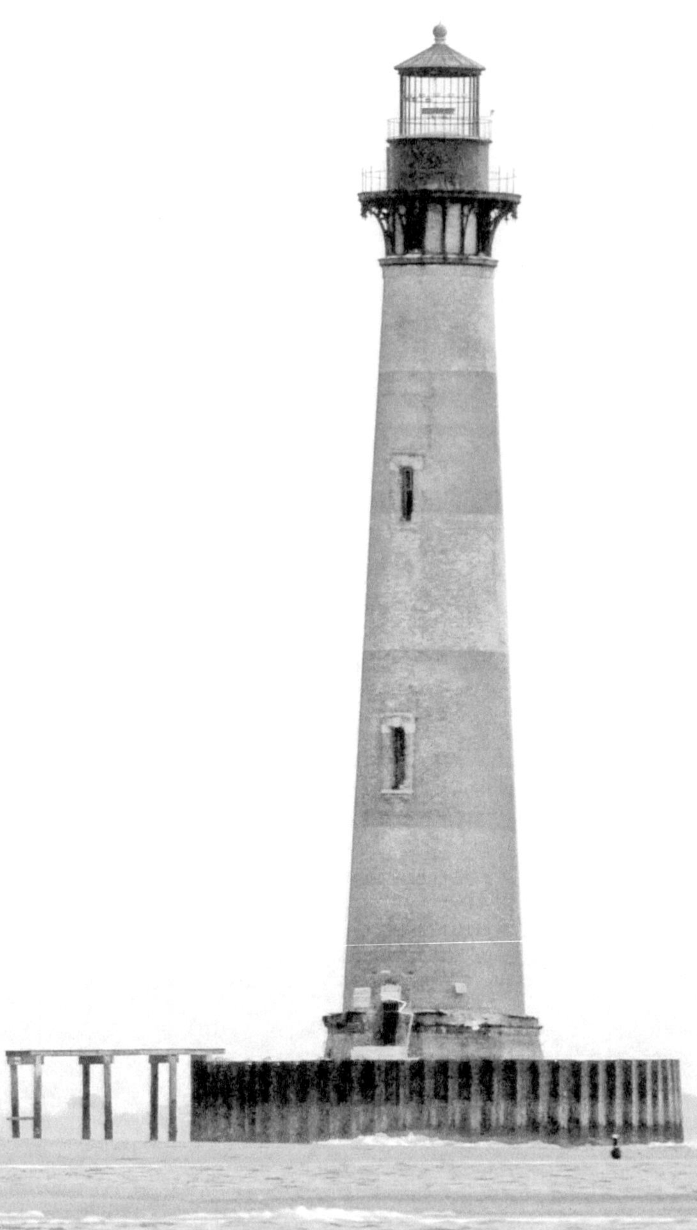

Morris Island Lighthouse

Lighthouse Inlet Heritage Preserve

Ravenel Bridge

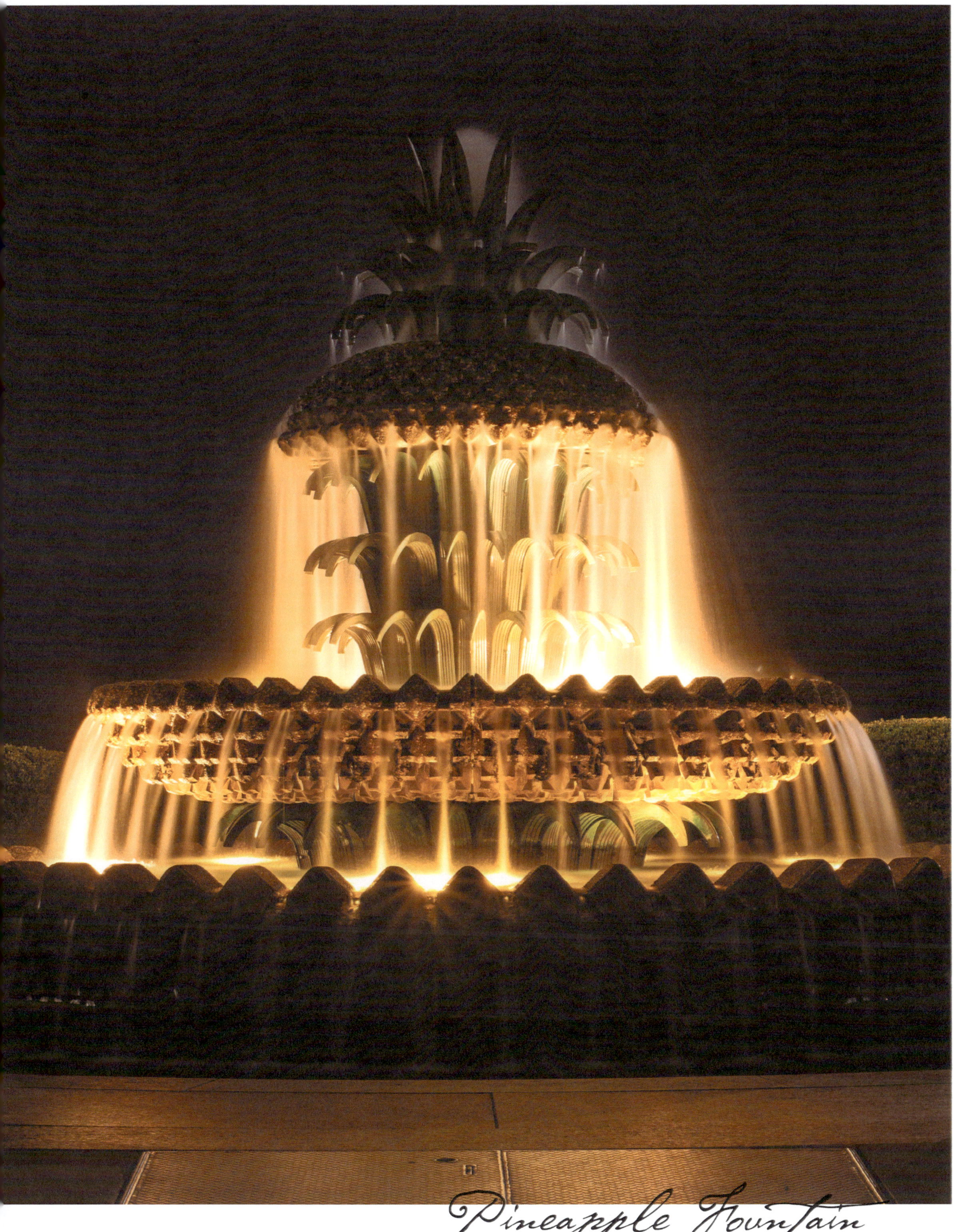

Pineapple Fountain

Shem Creek

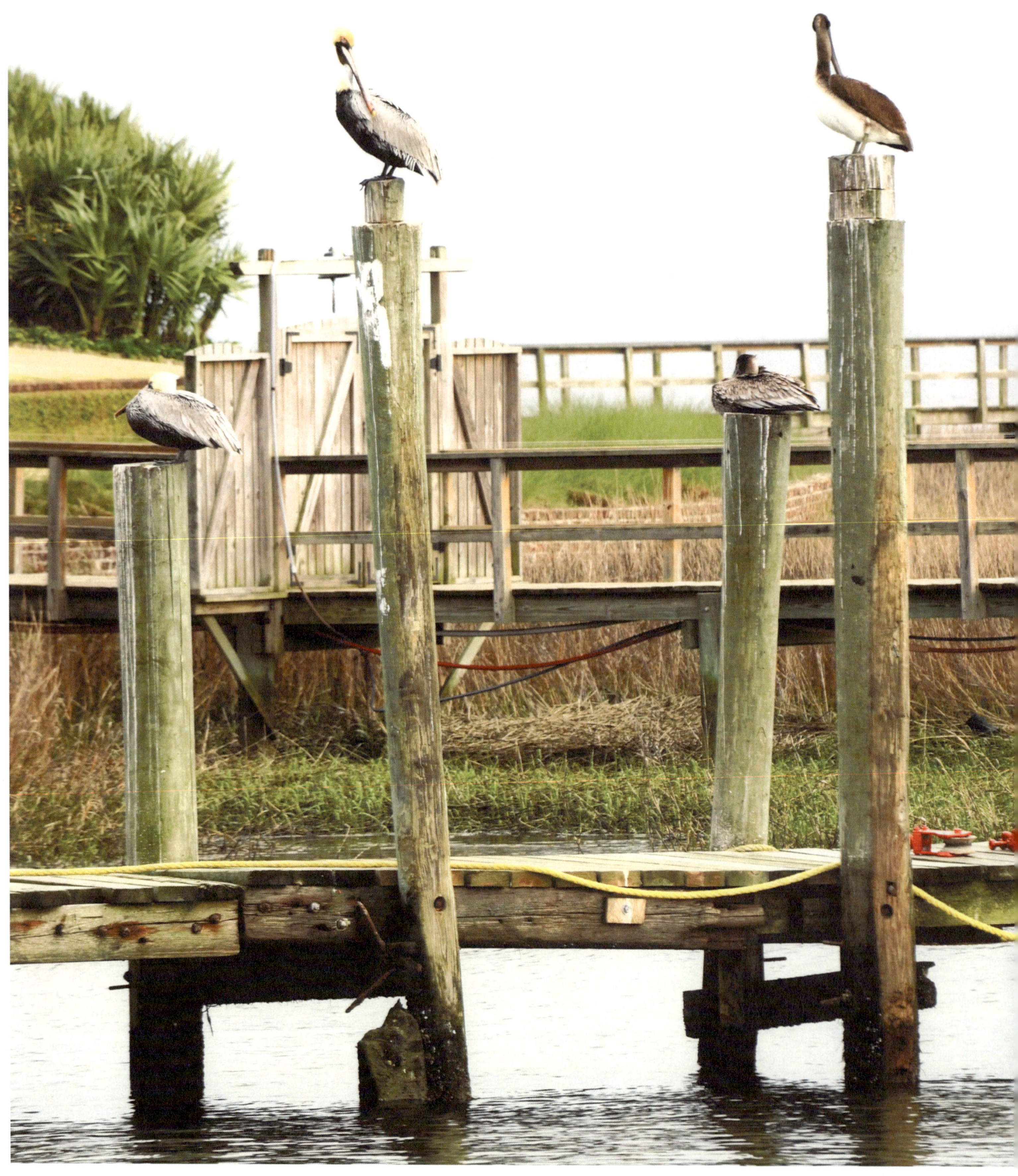

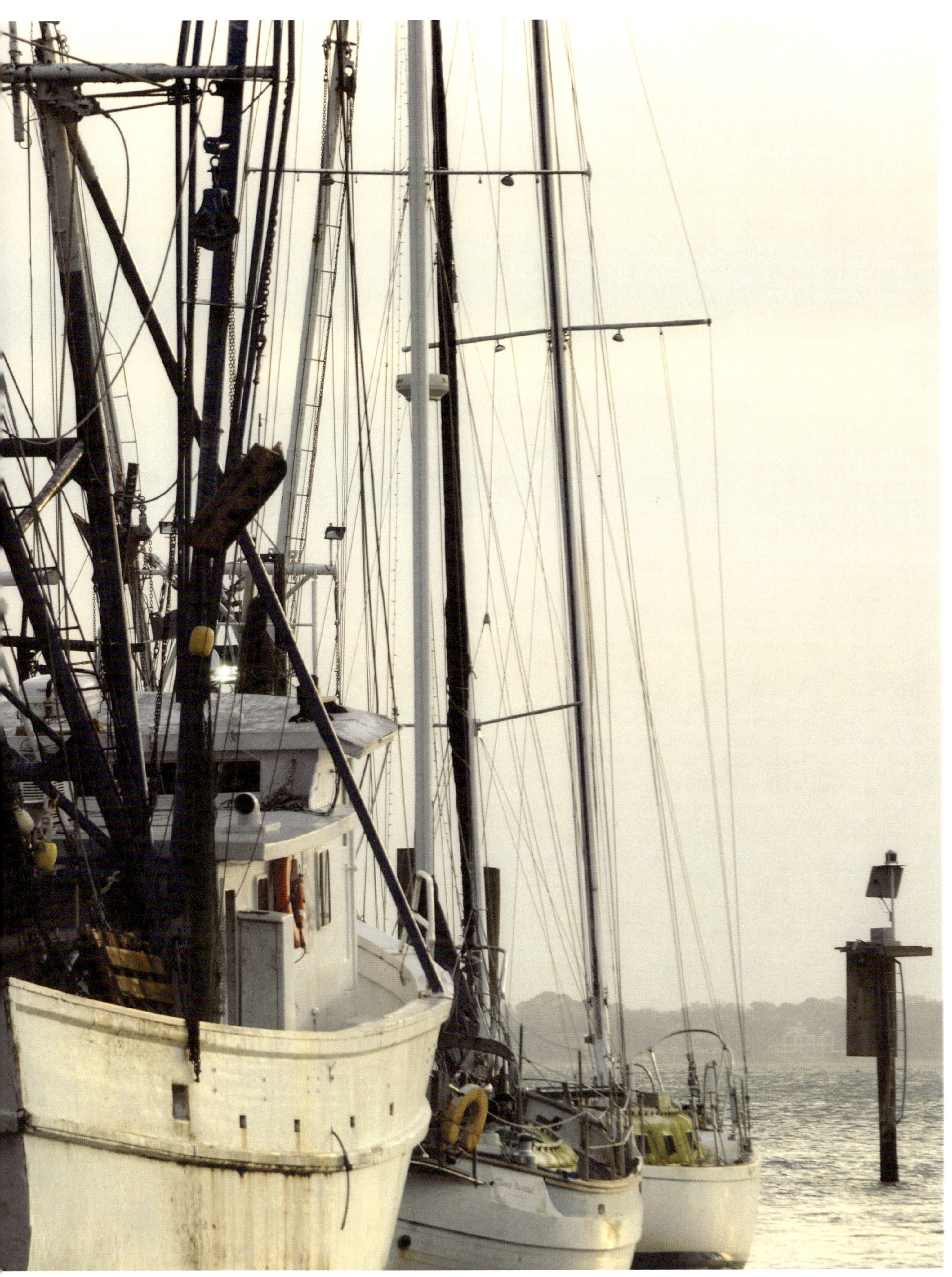

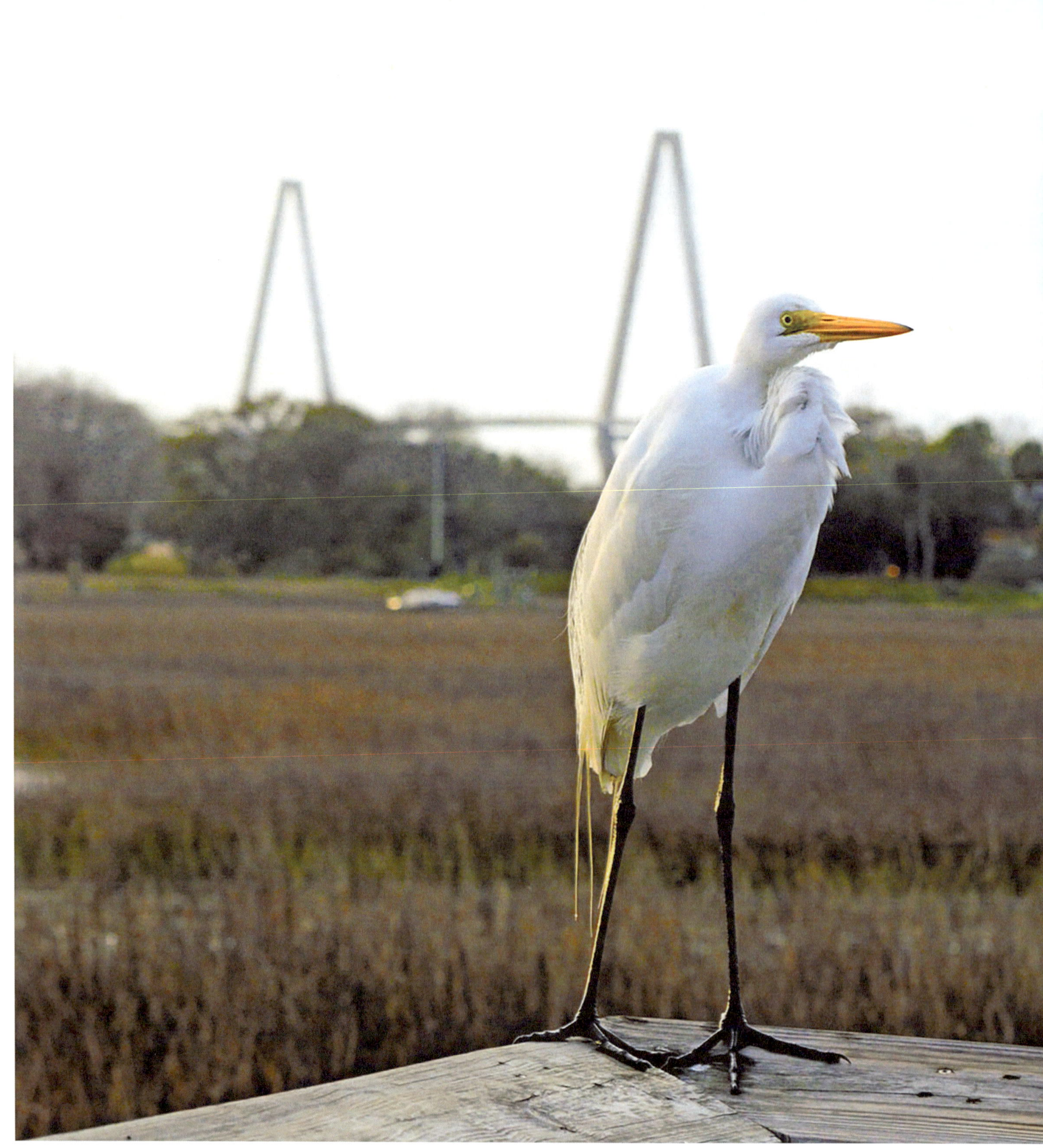

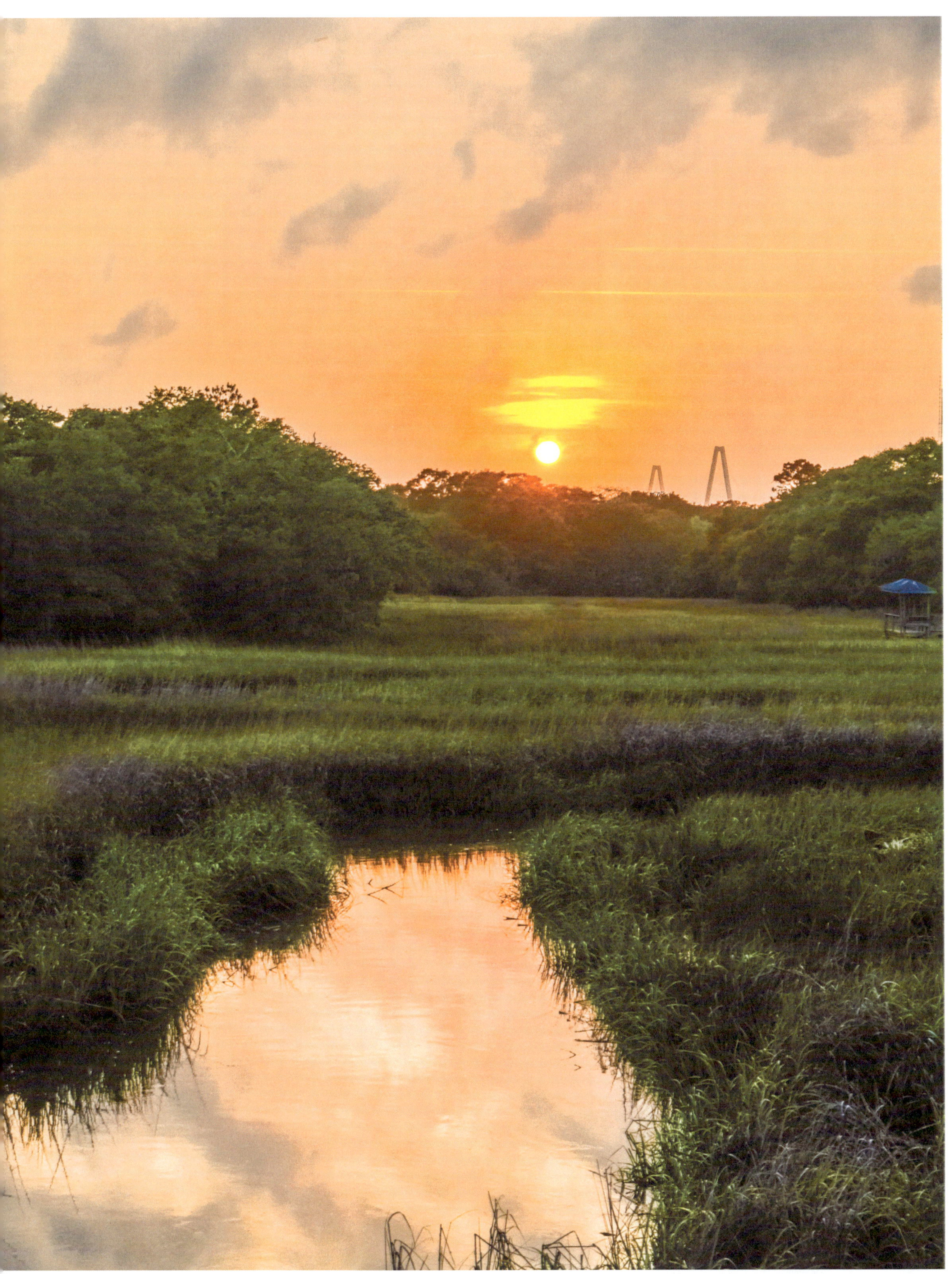

Hampton Park

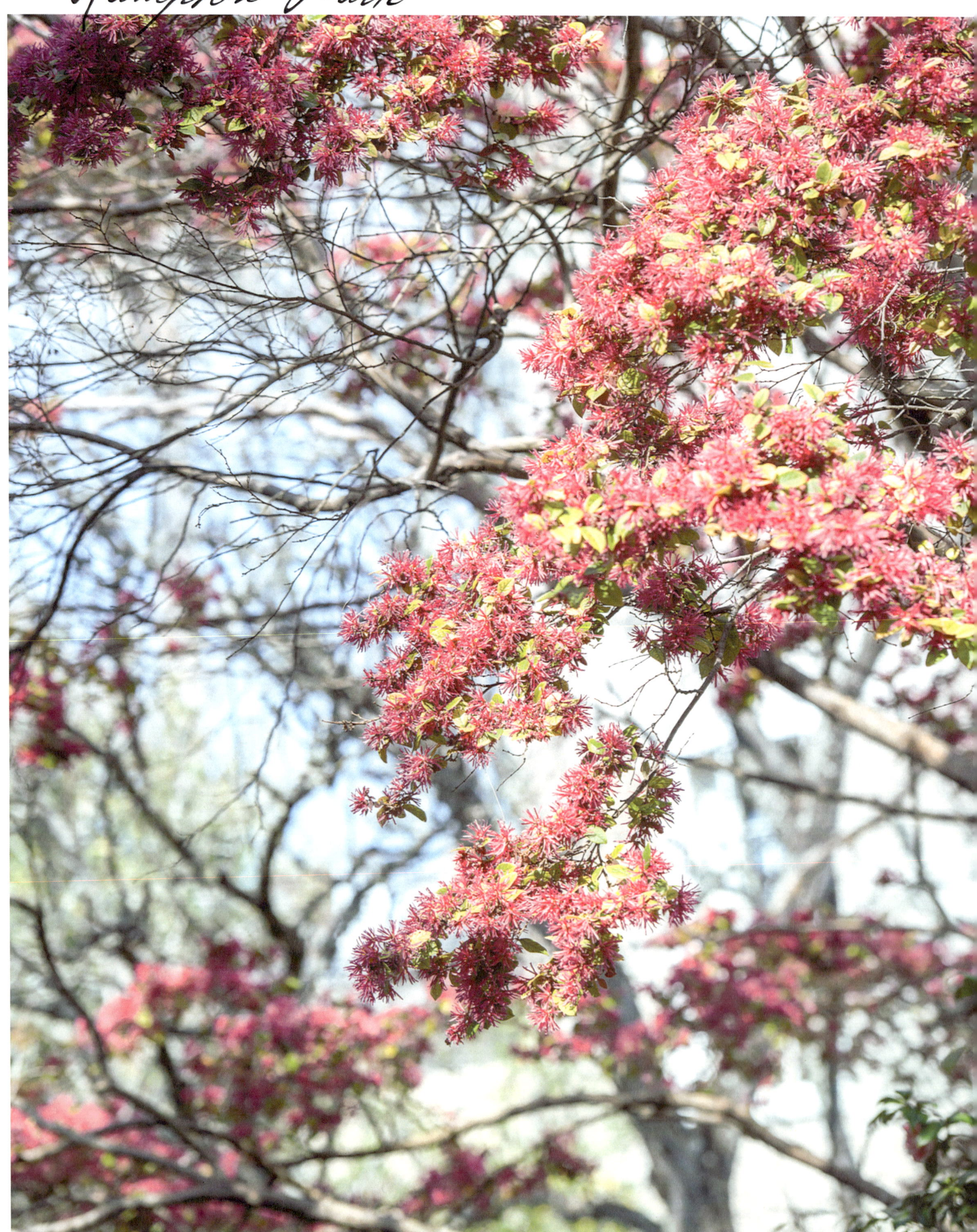

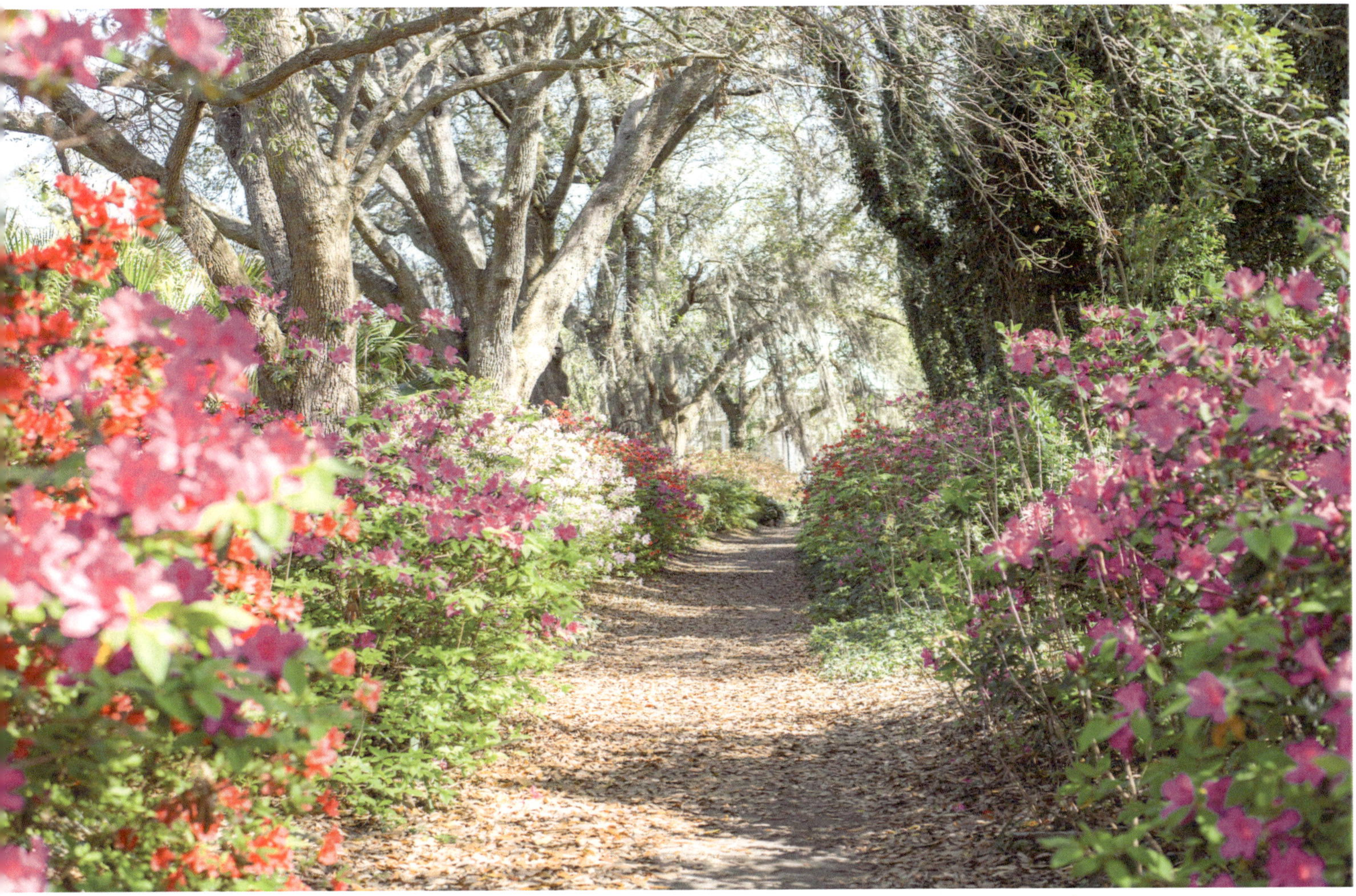

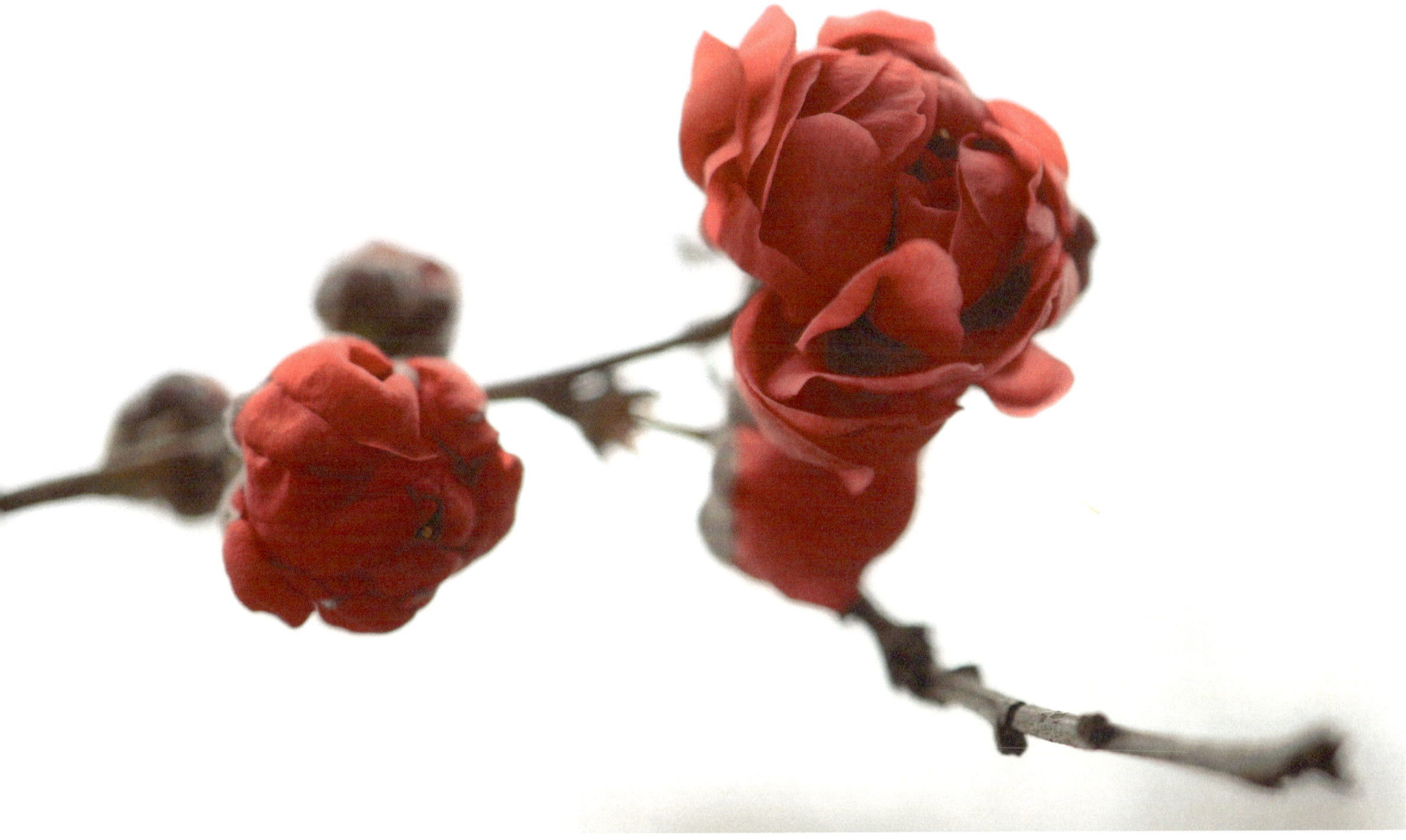

Elliott Street

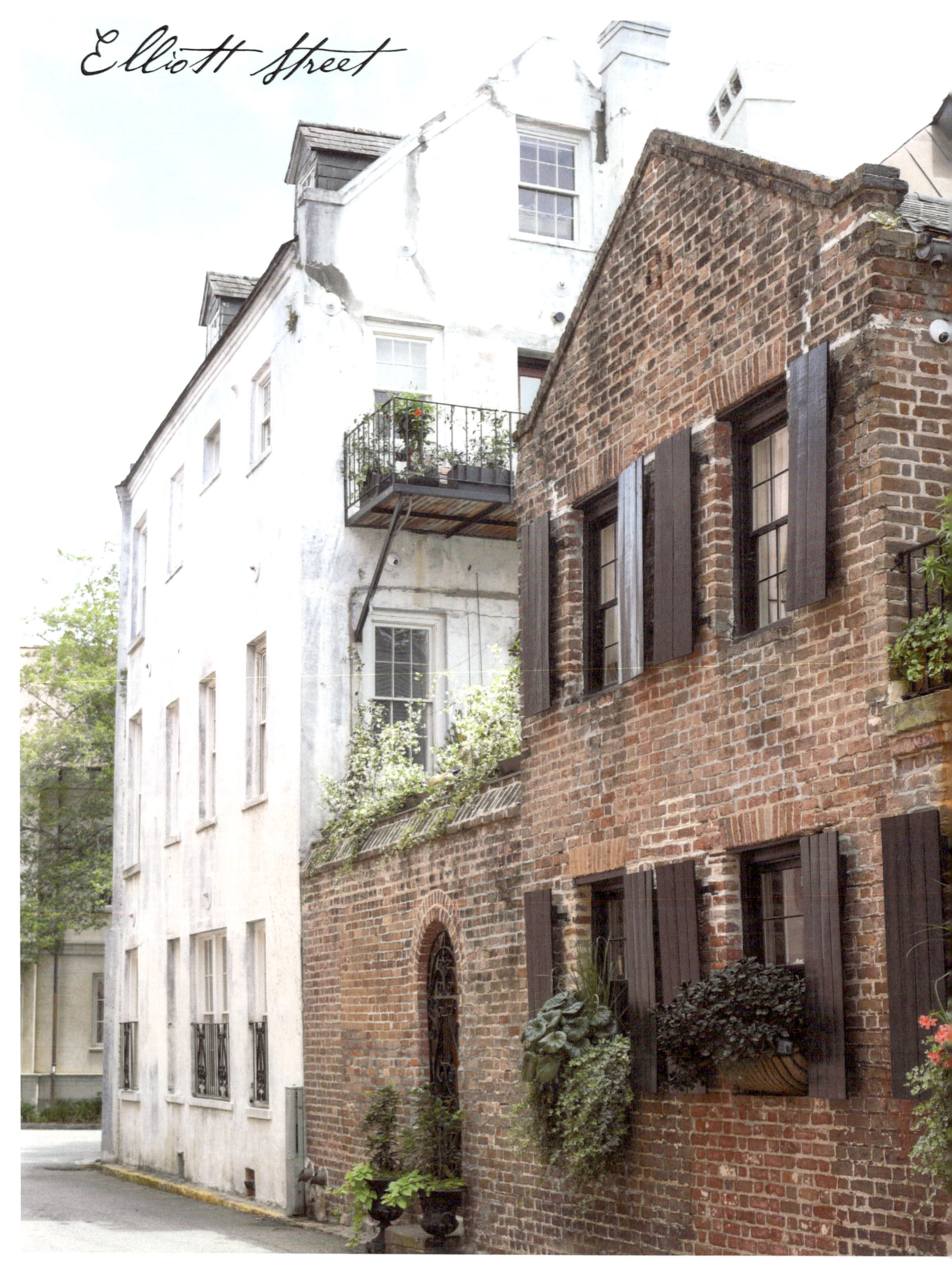

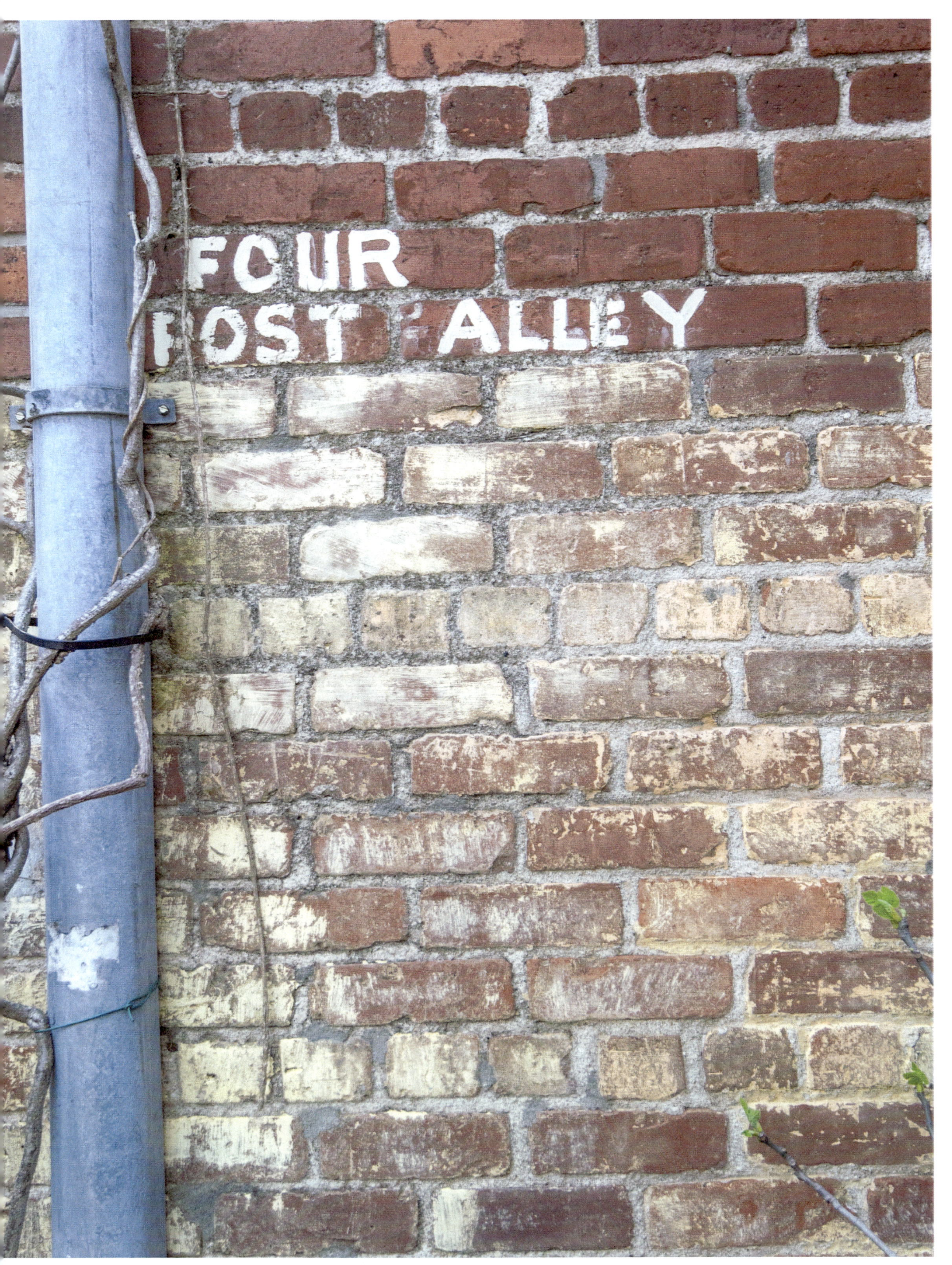
FOUR
POST ALLEY

Downtown Charleston

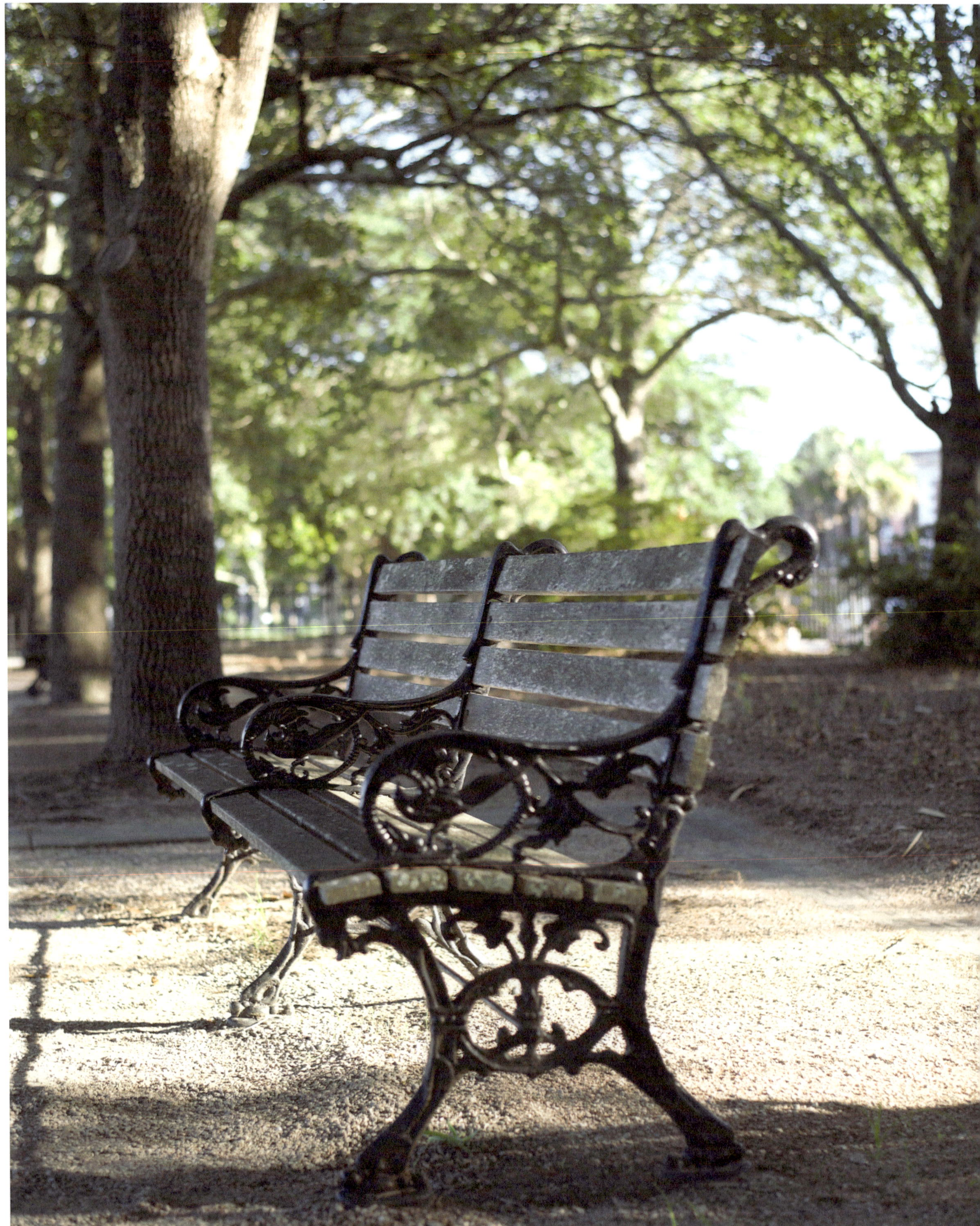

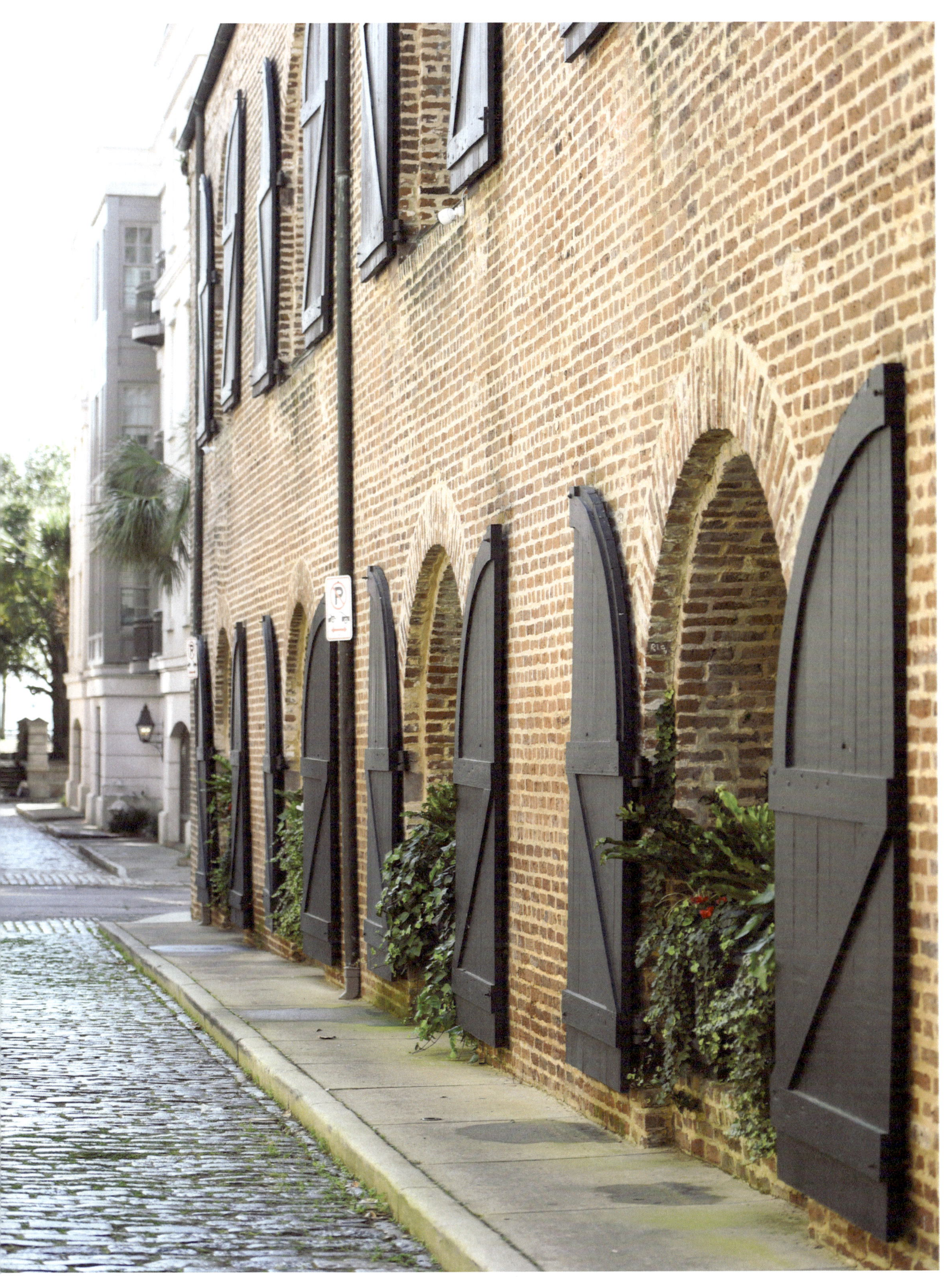

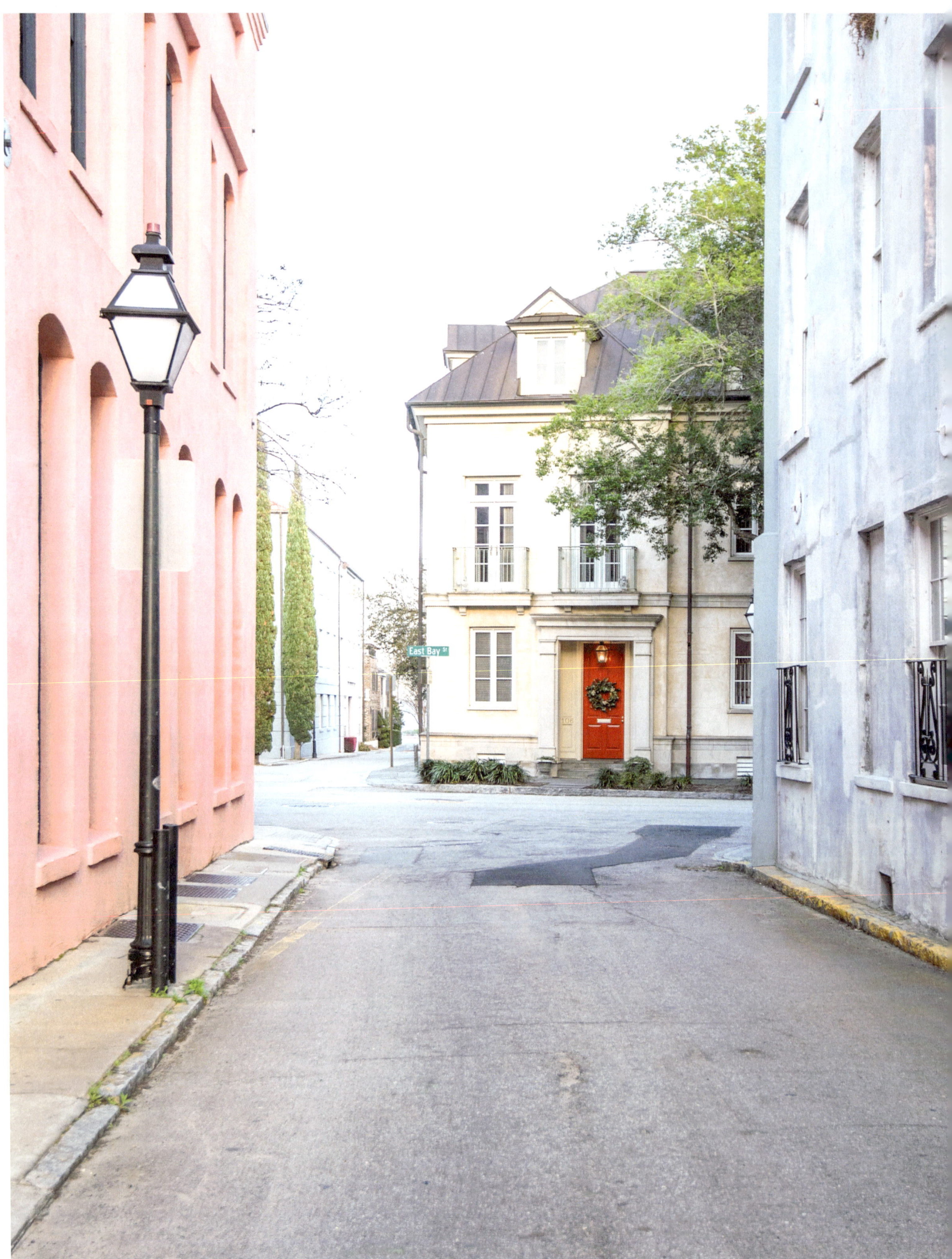
East Bay St

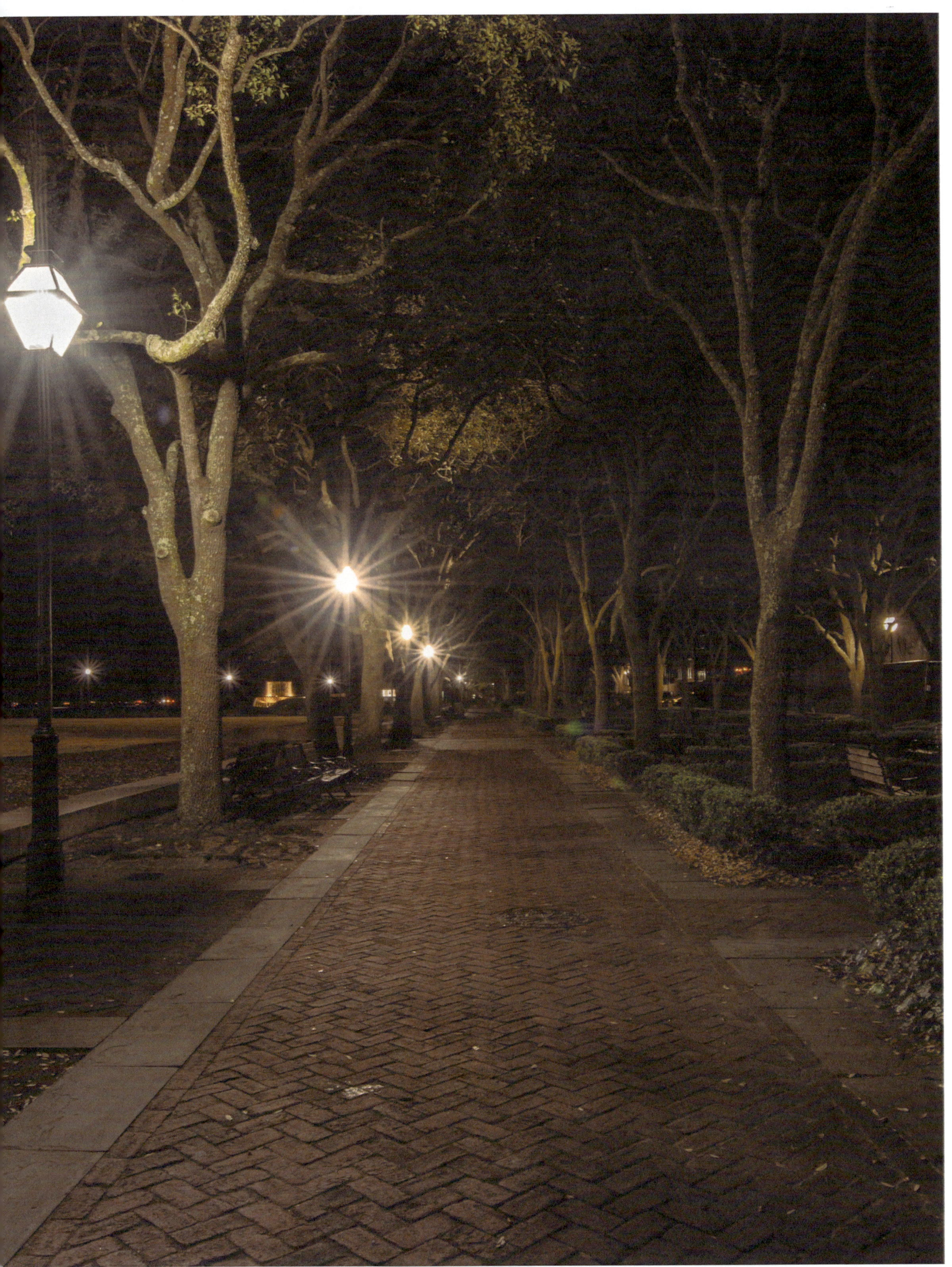

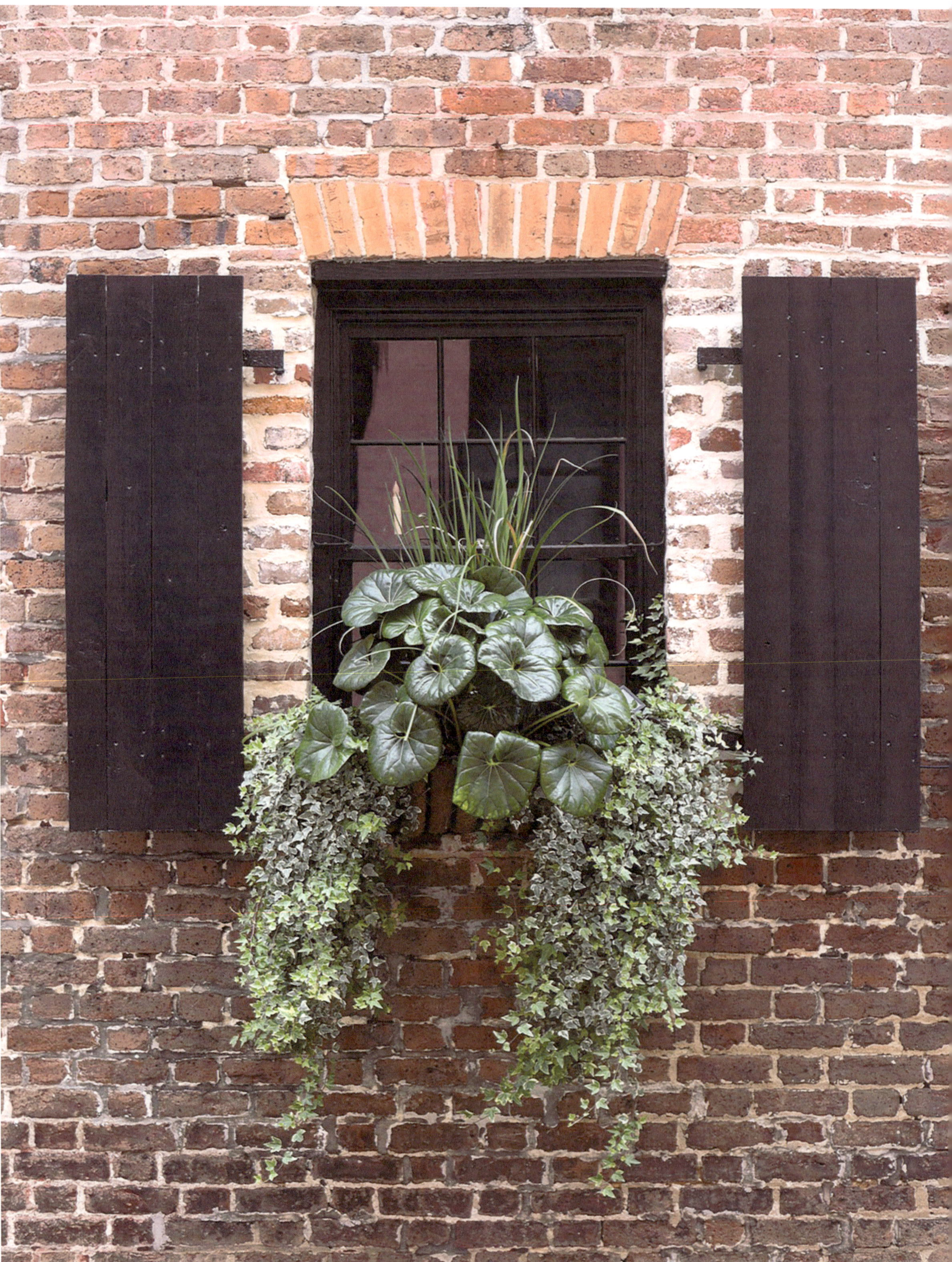

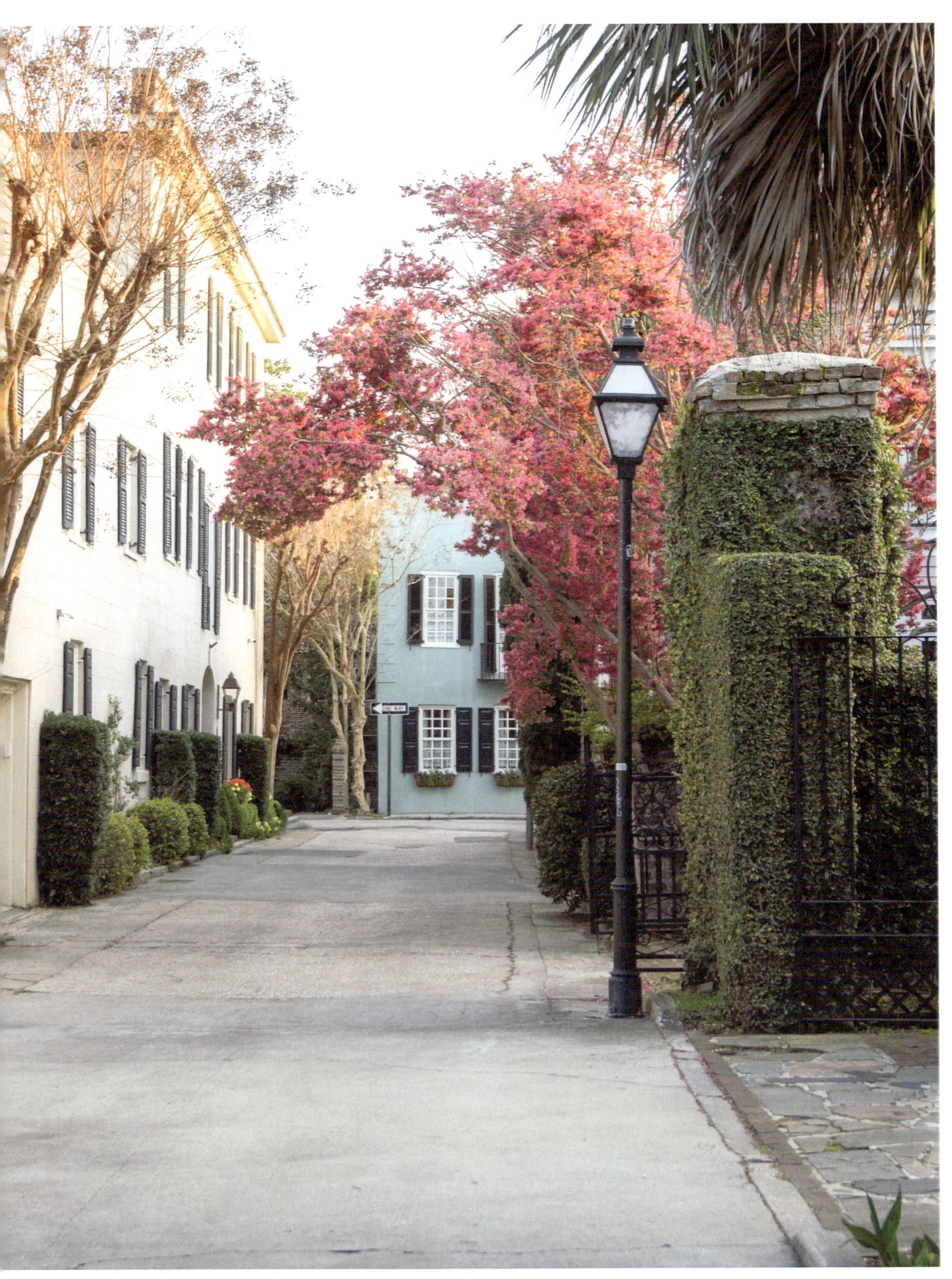
ONE WAY

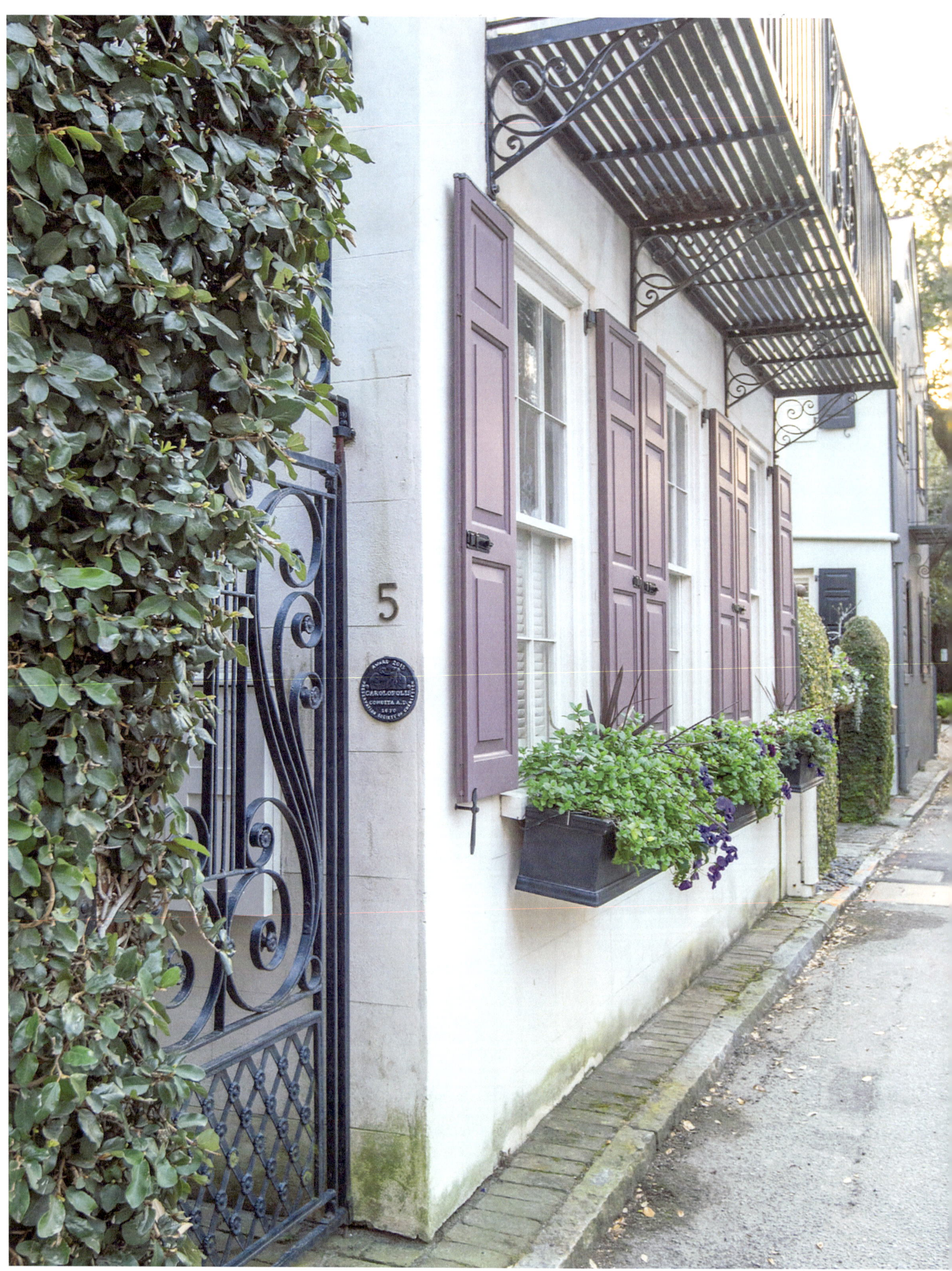
5
CAROLOPOLIS
1670

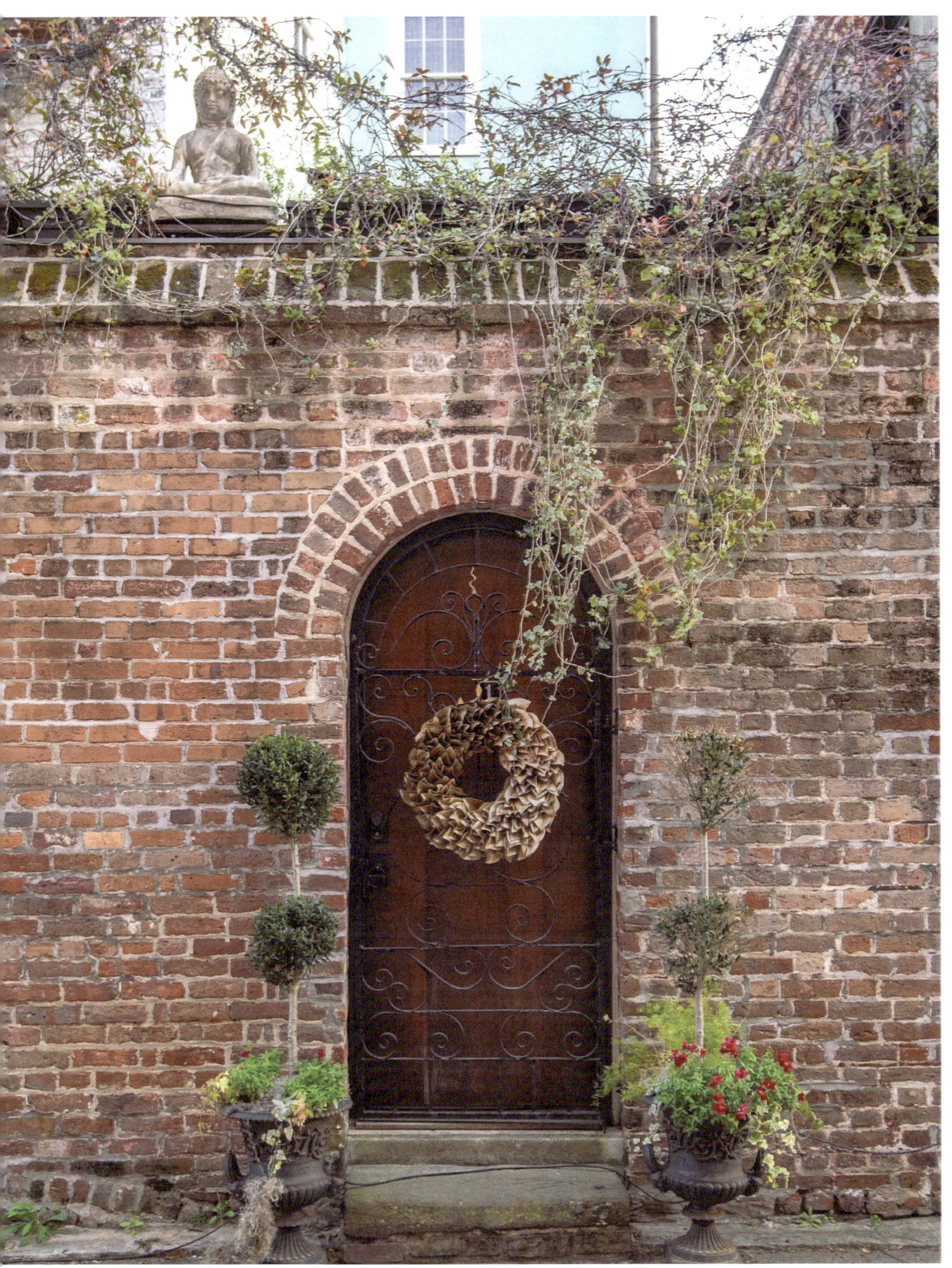

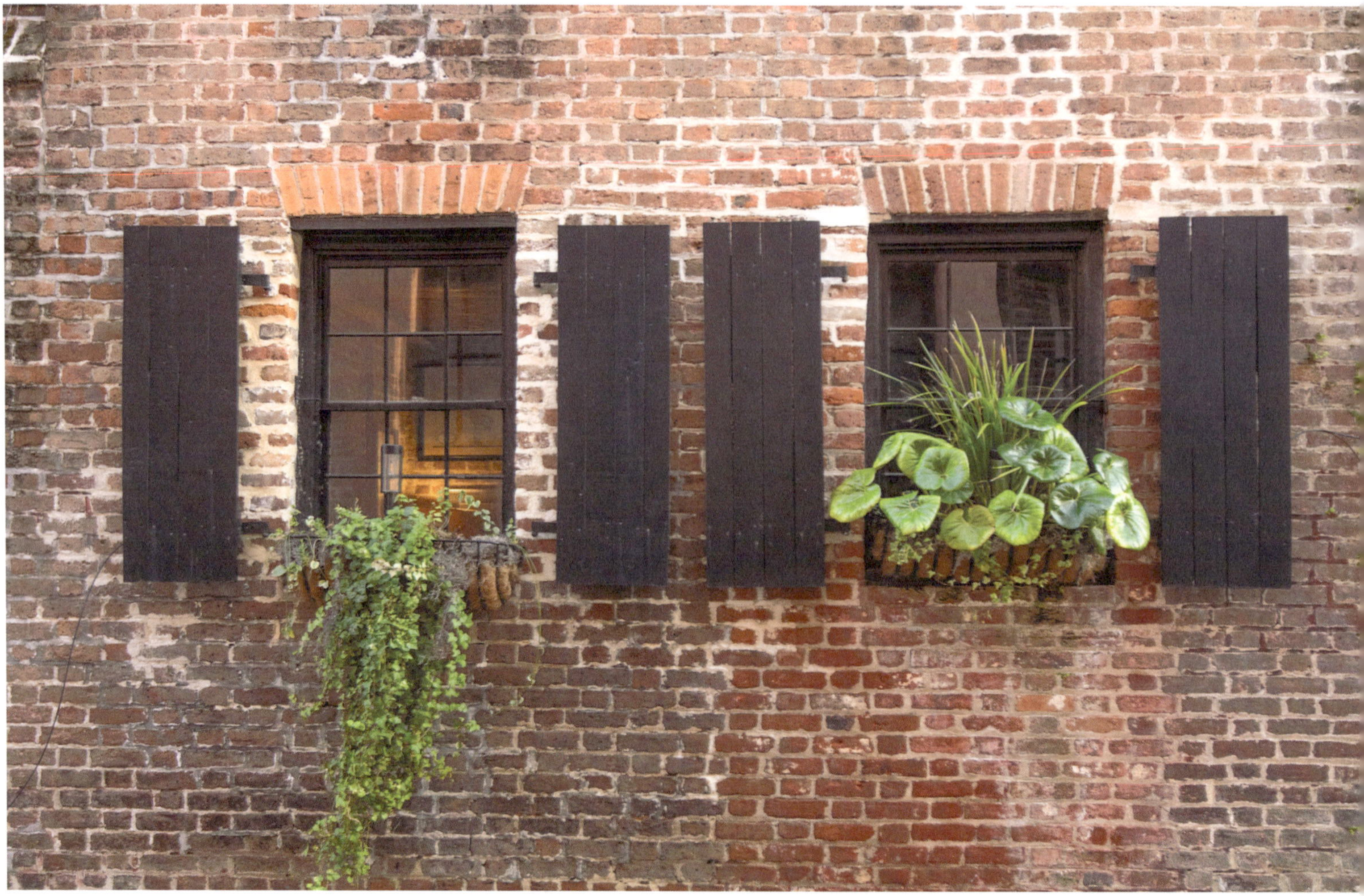

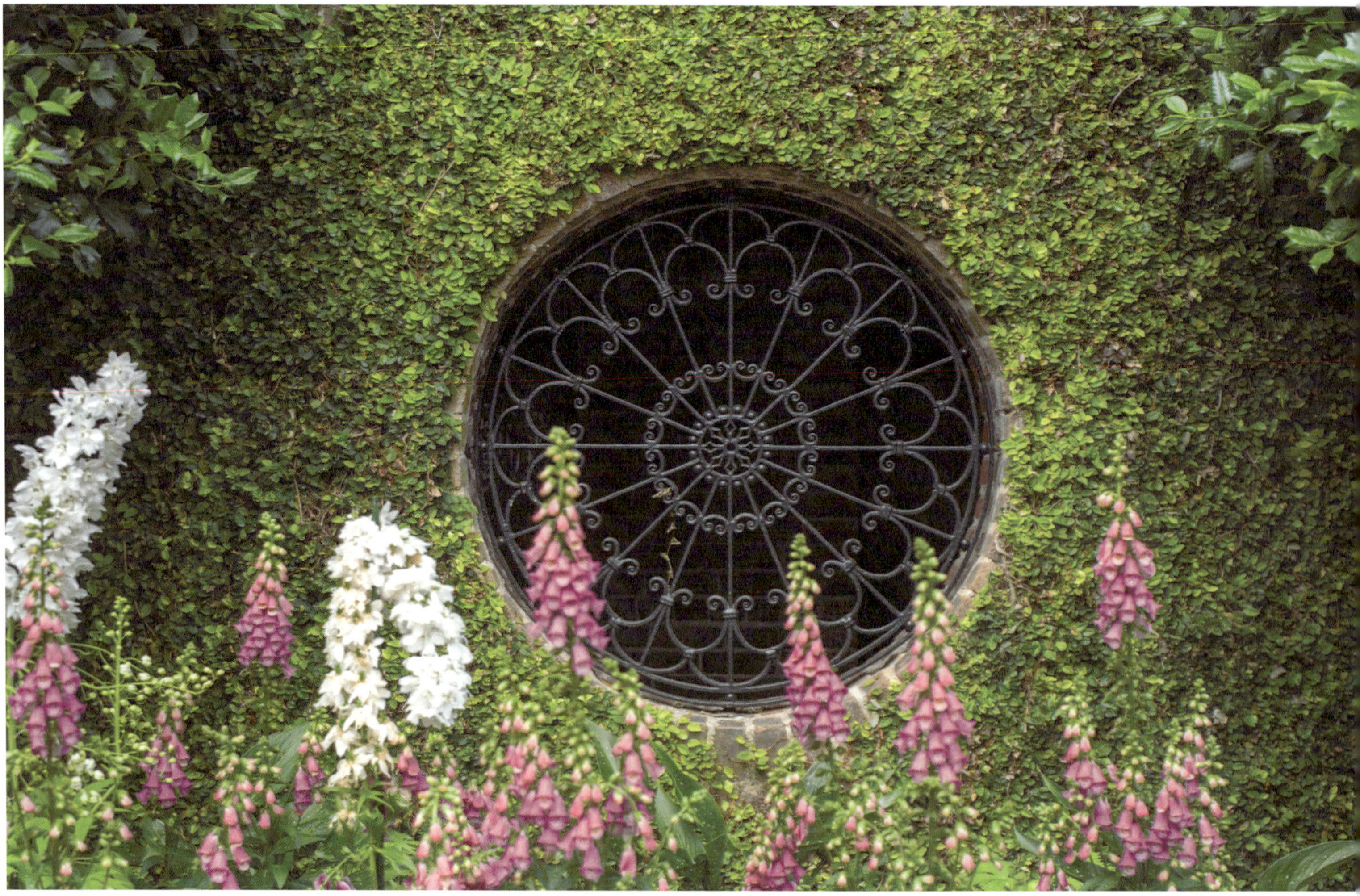

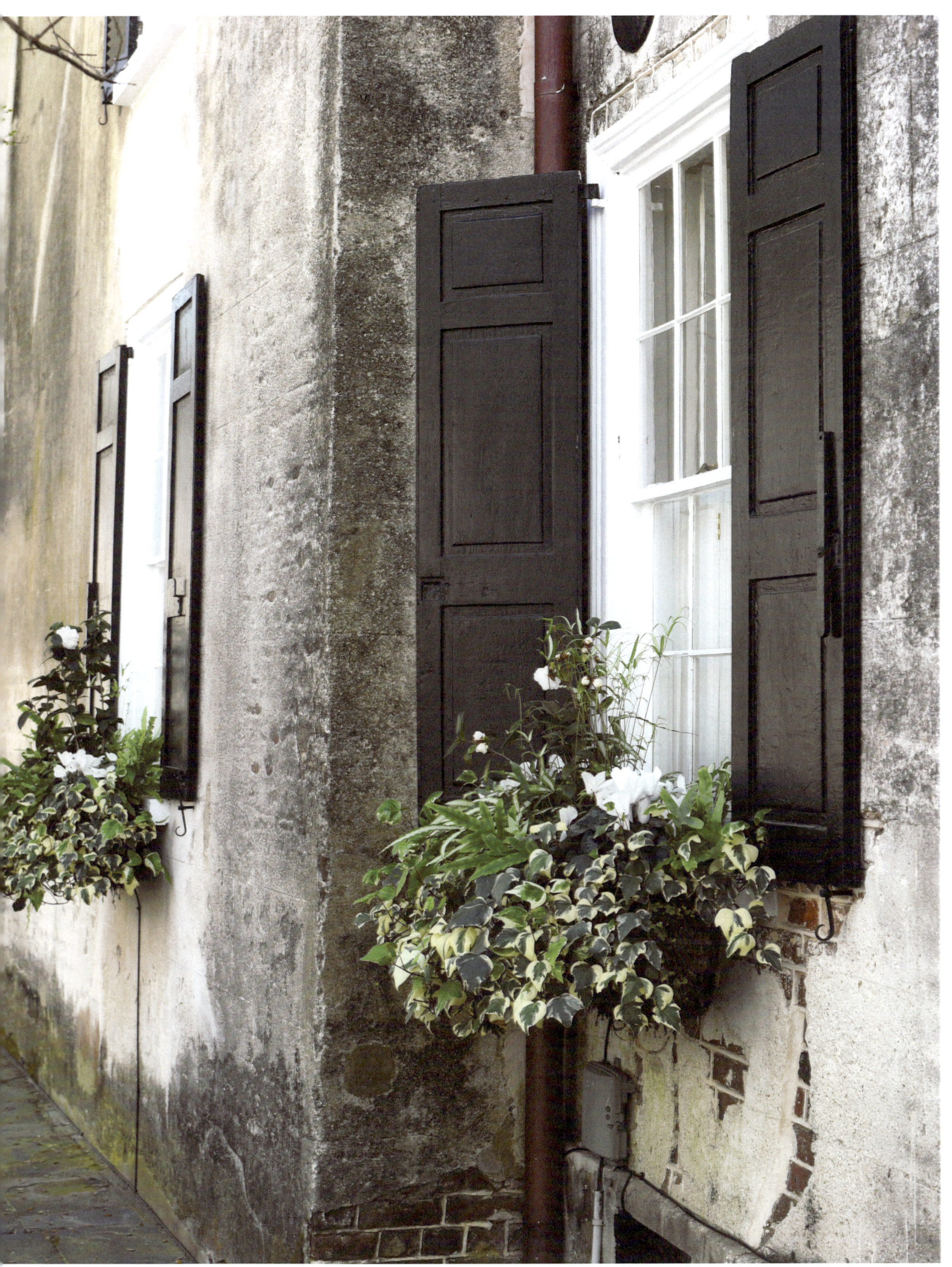

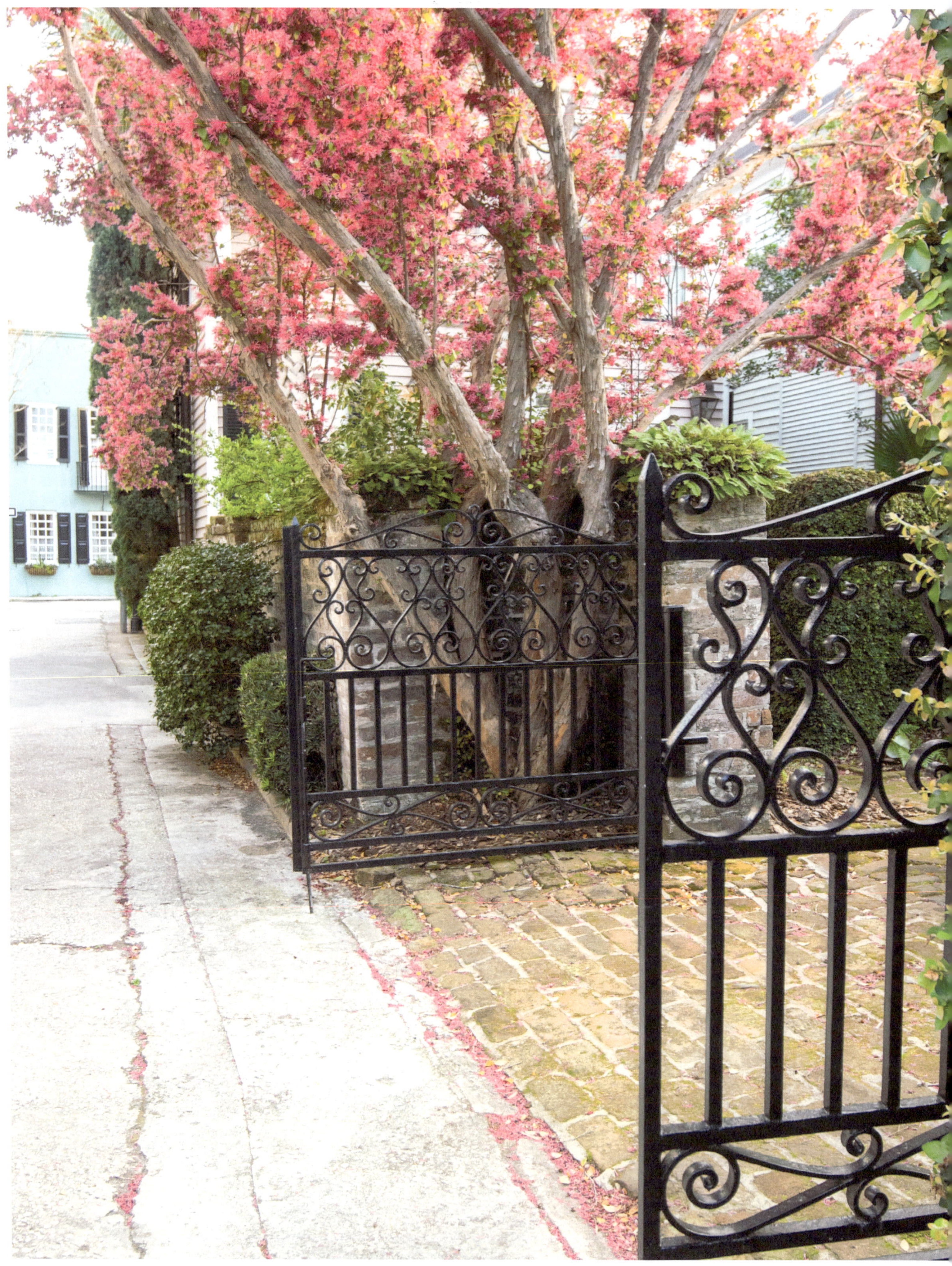

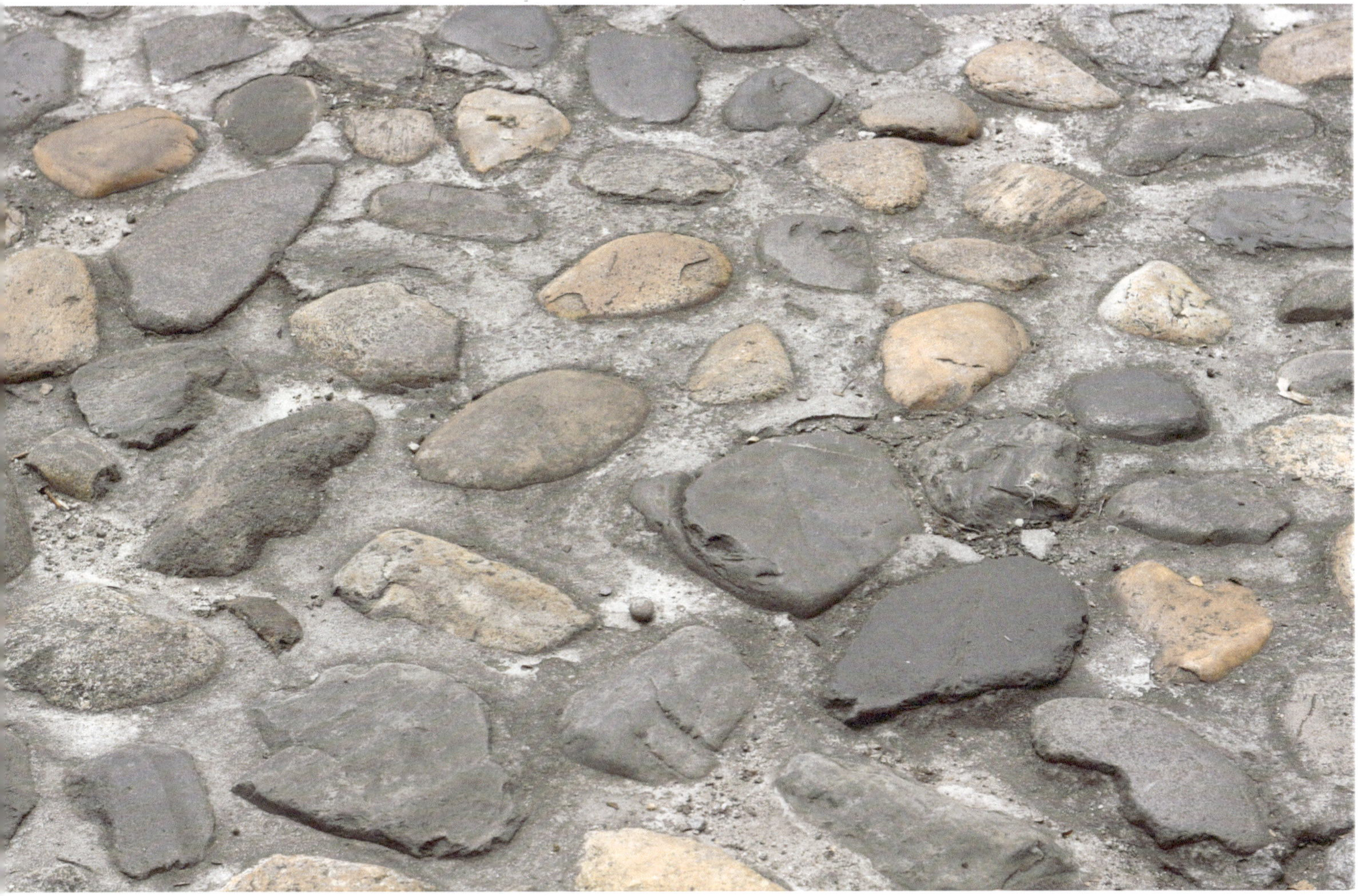

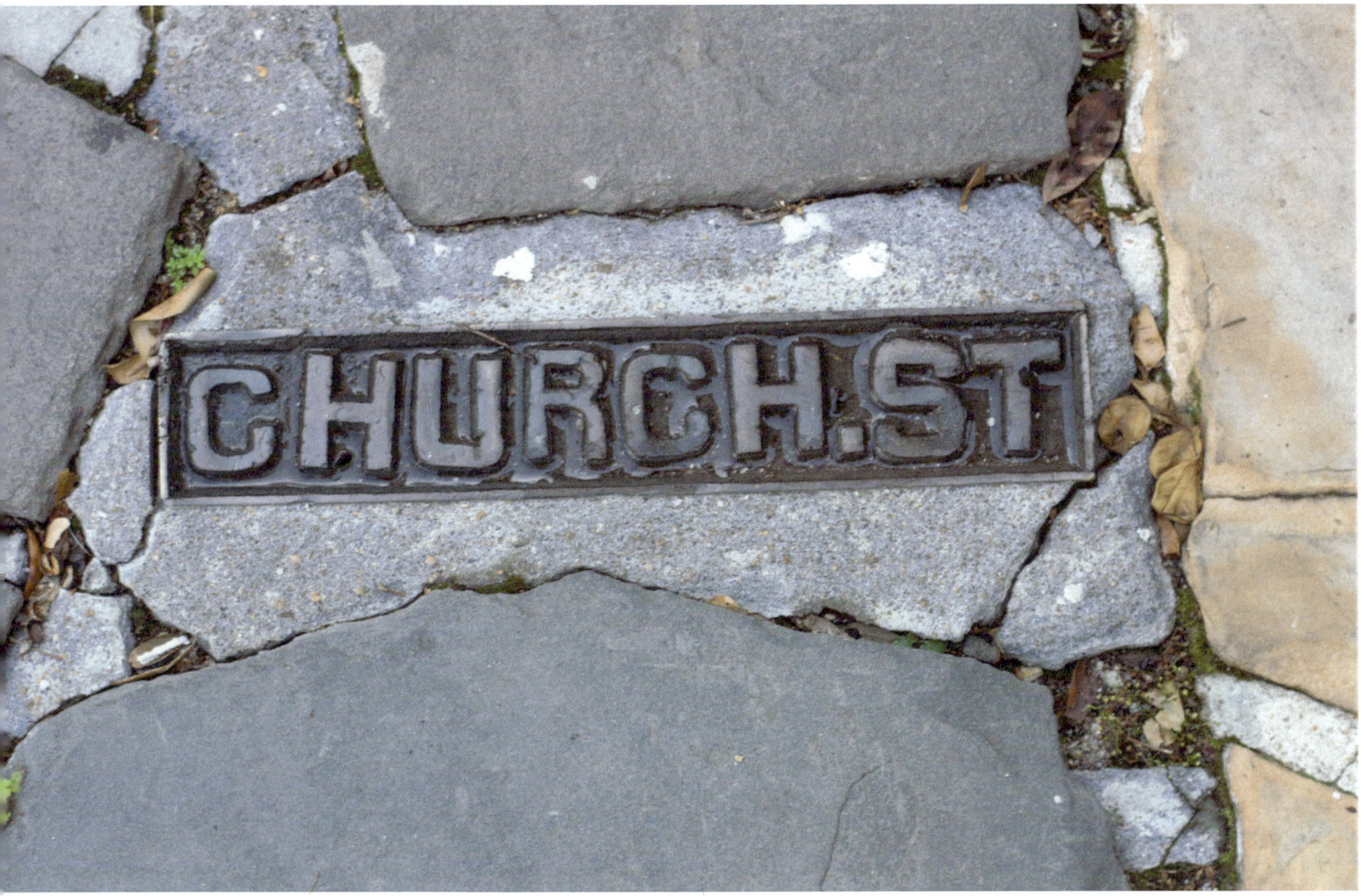

CHURCH.ST

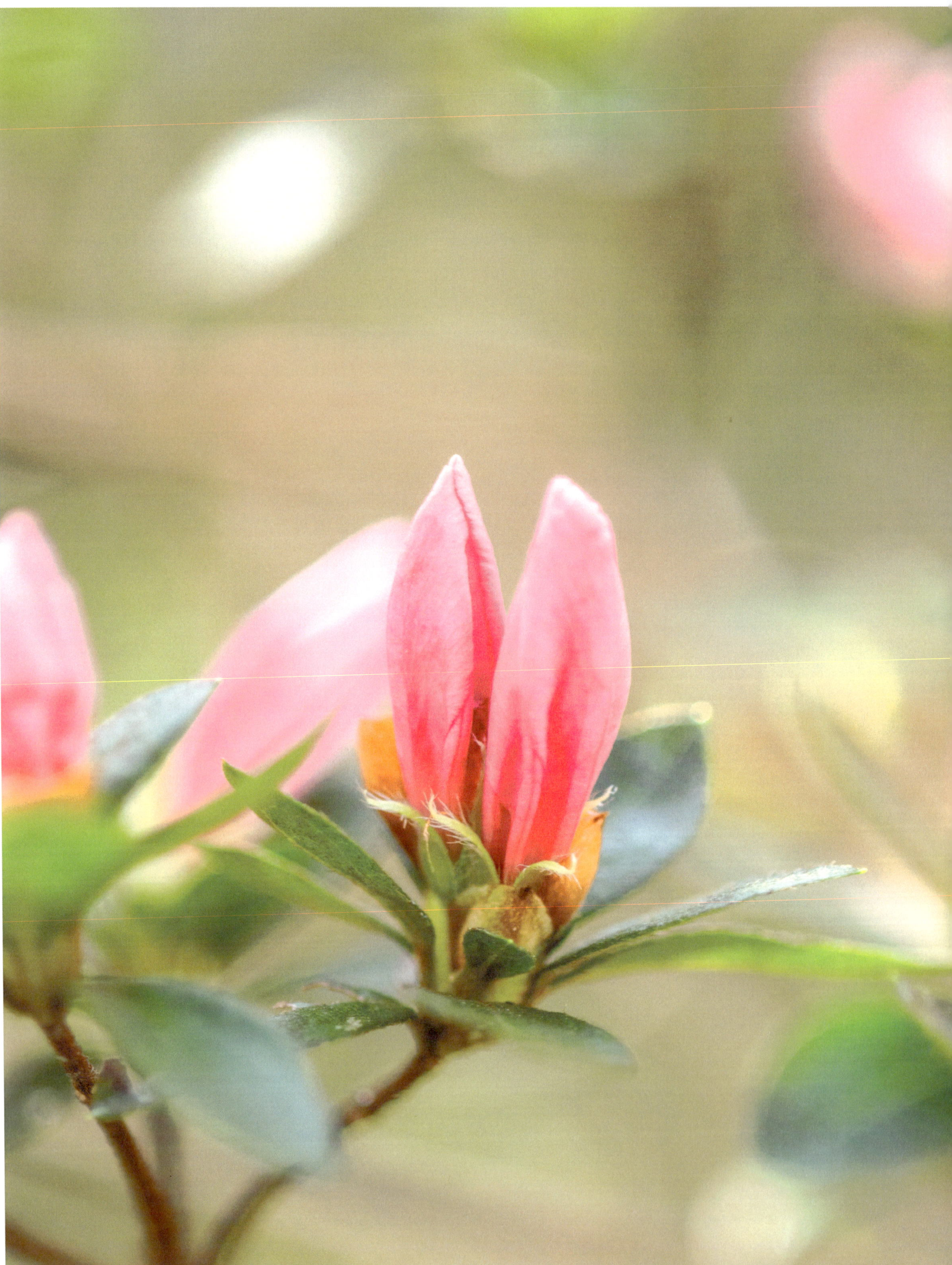

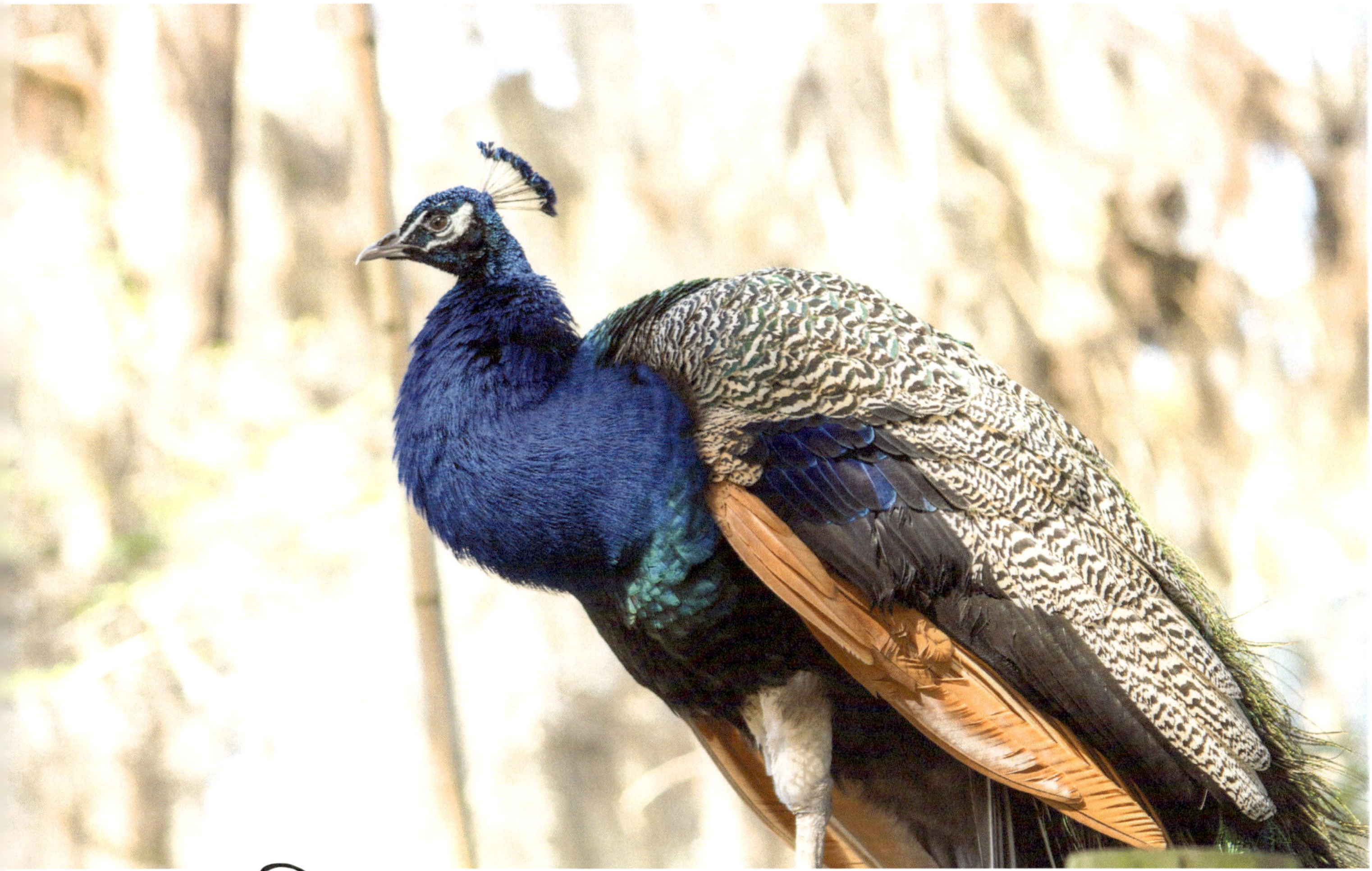

Magnolia Plantation & Gardens

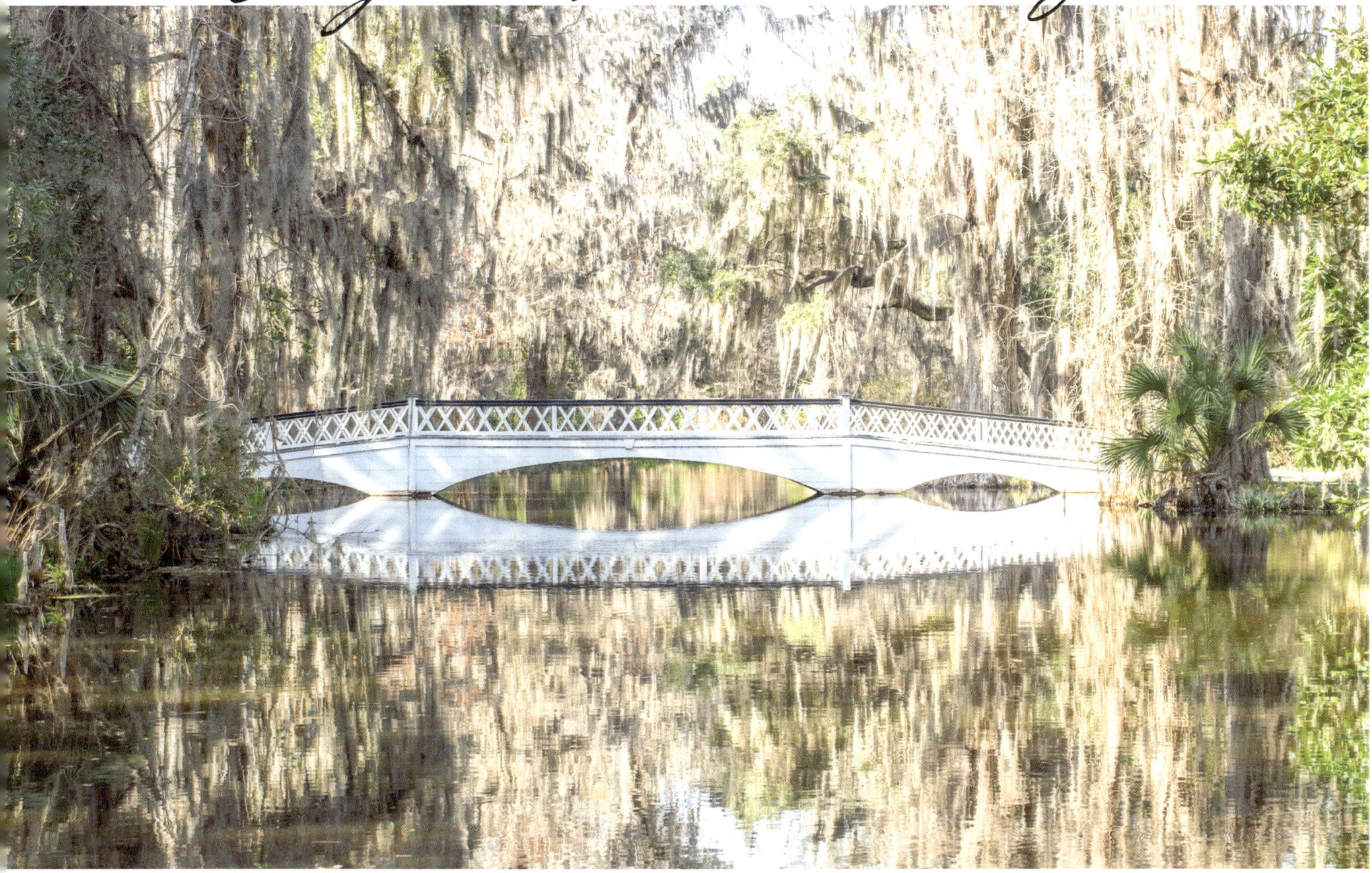

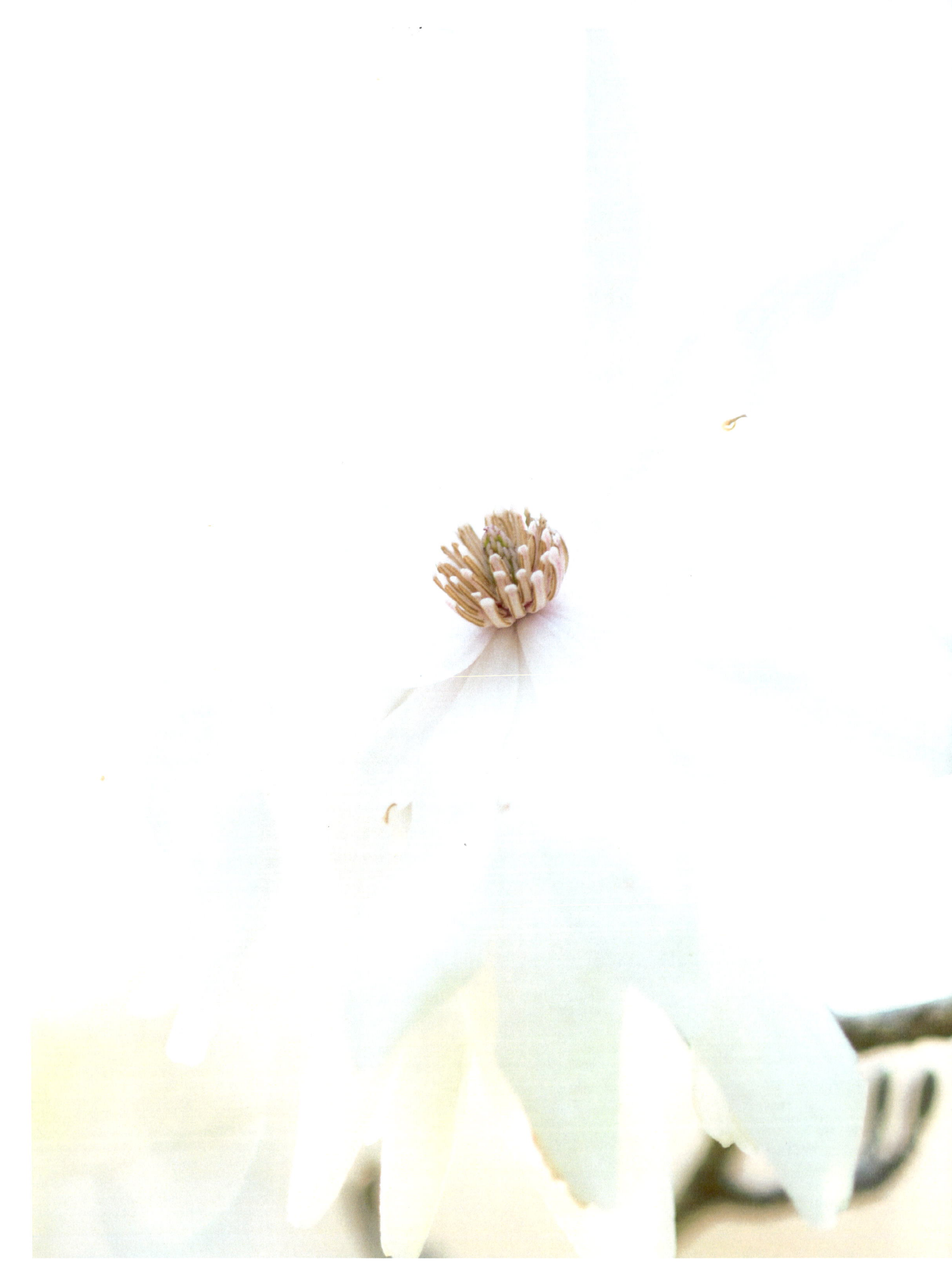

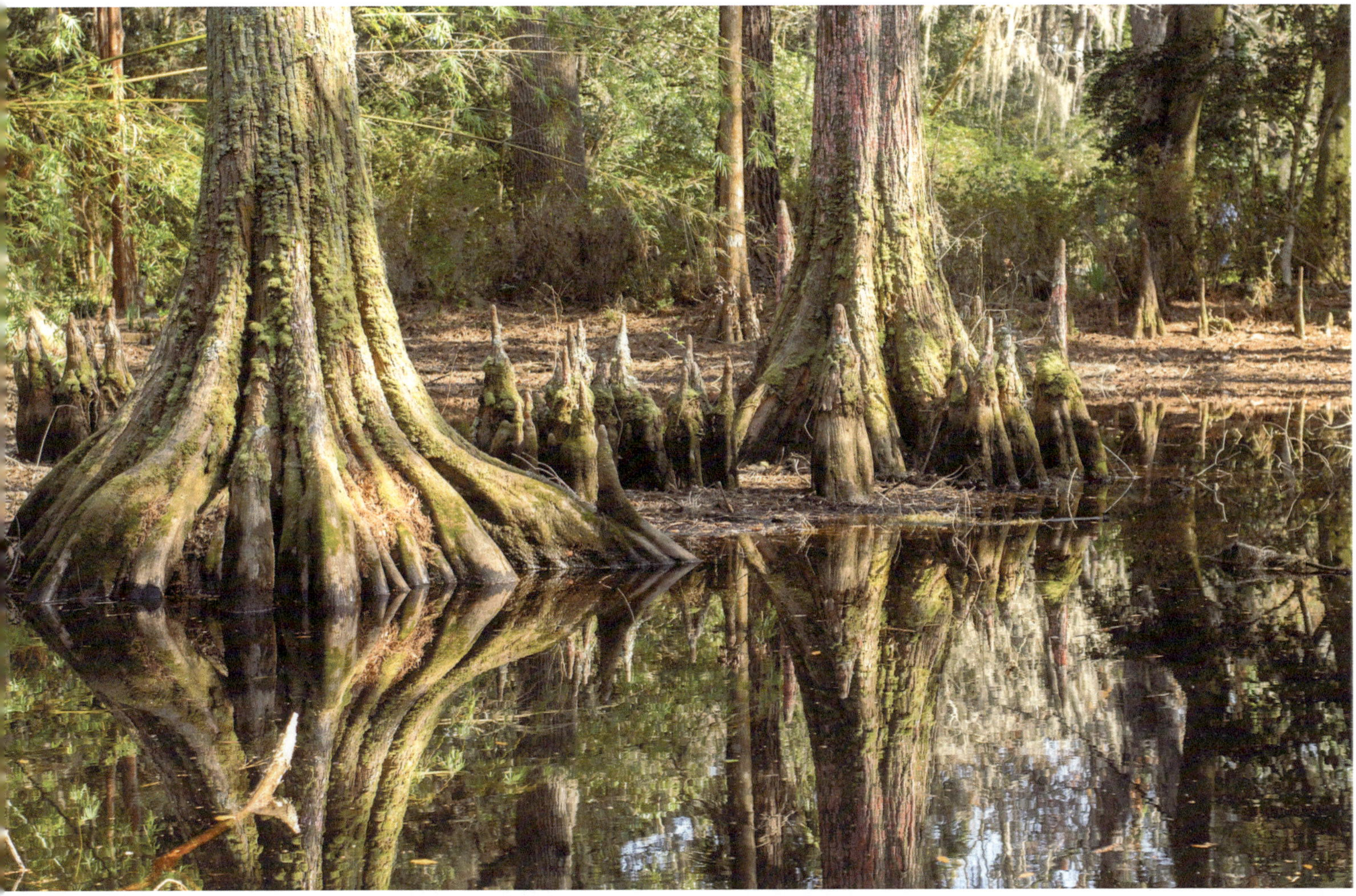

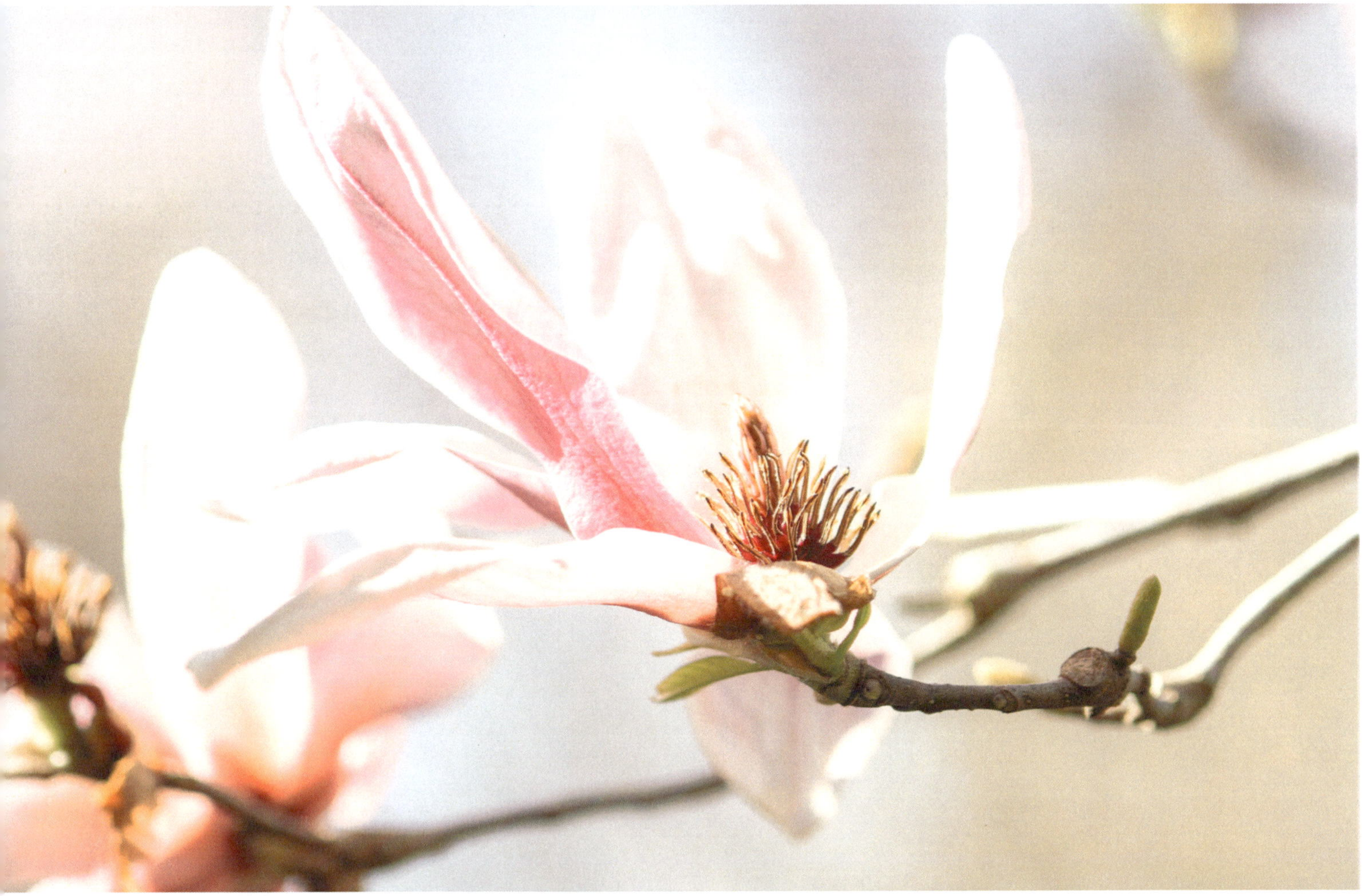

Charleston Tea Plantation

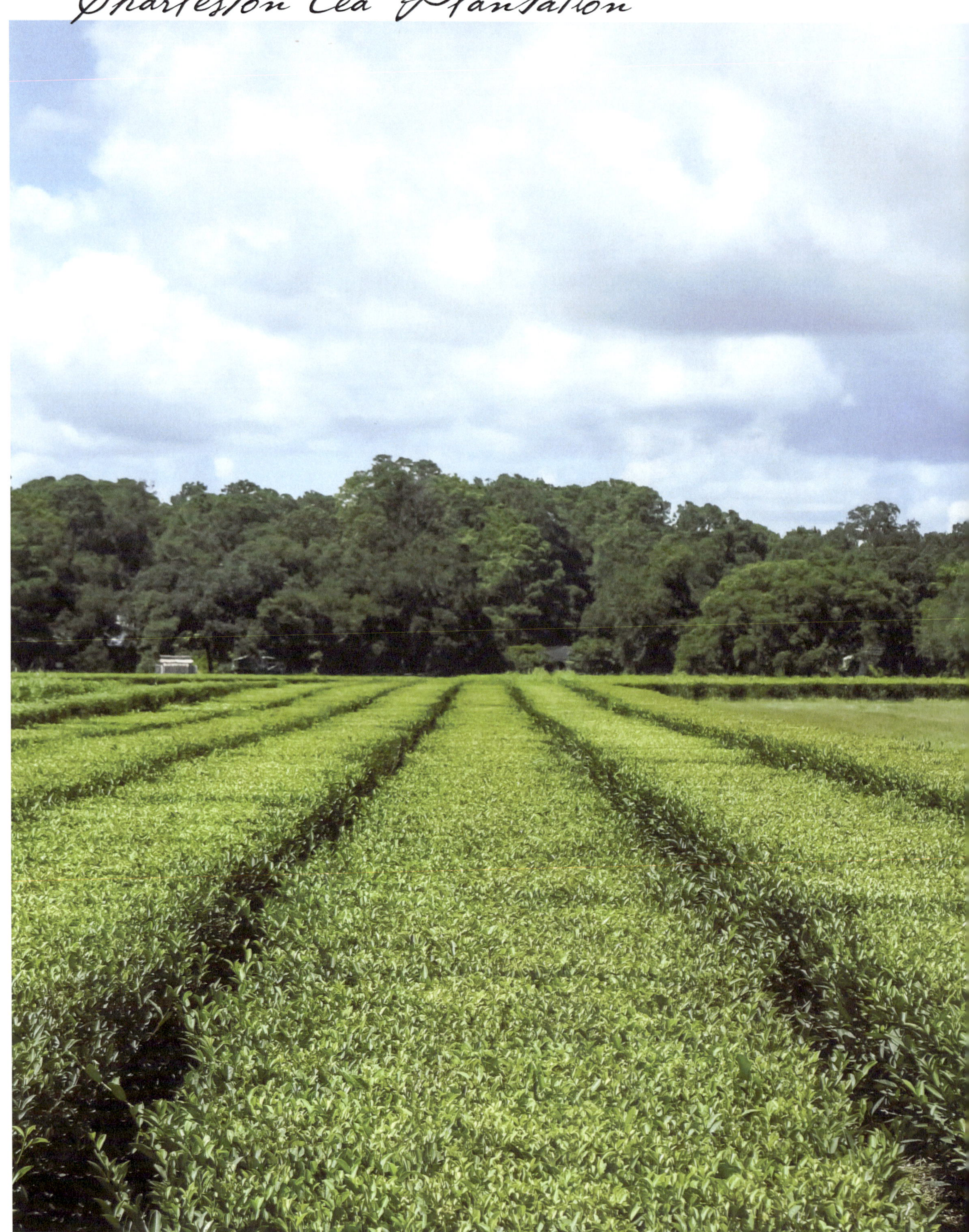

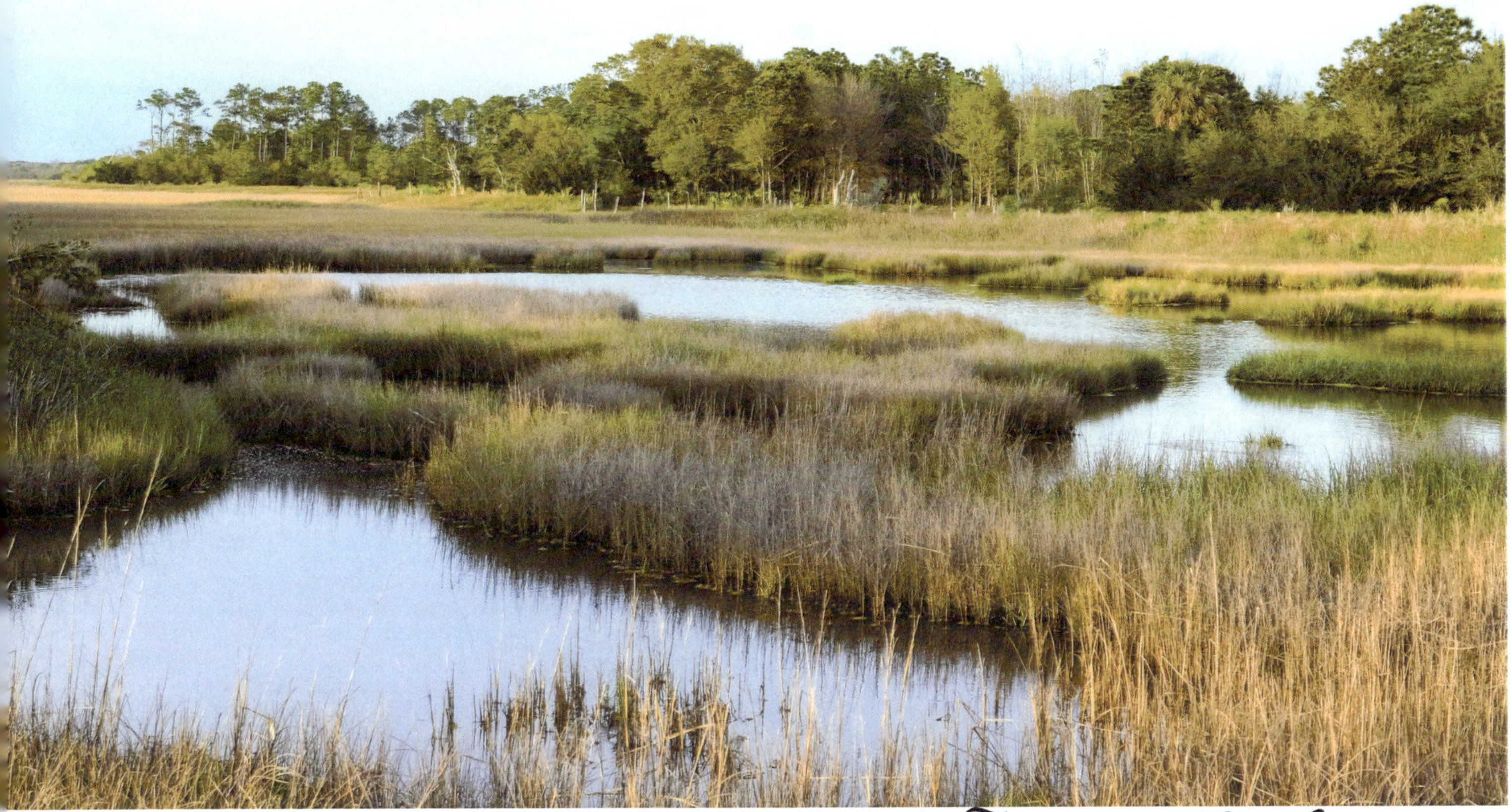

James Island

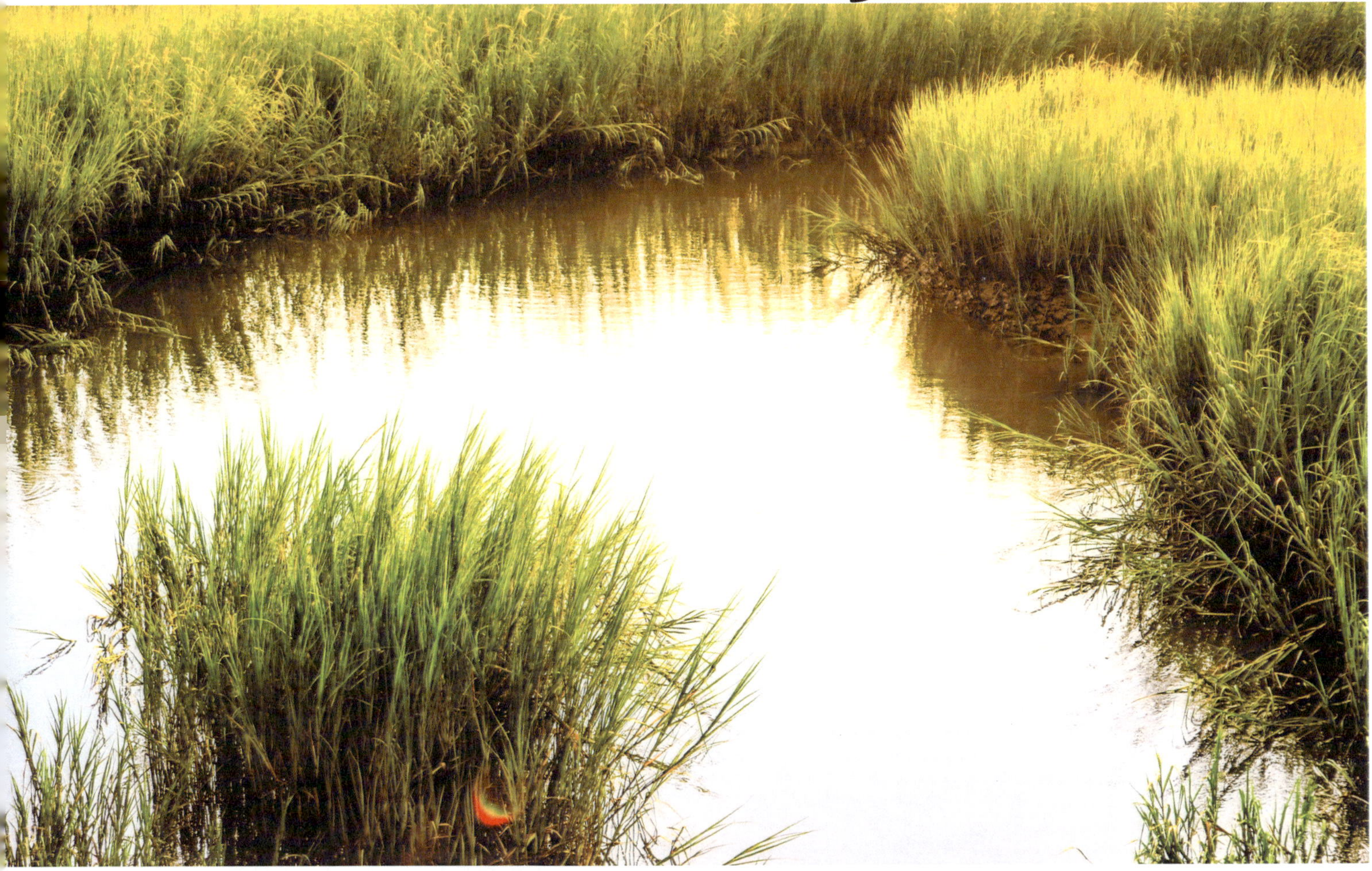

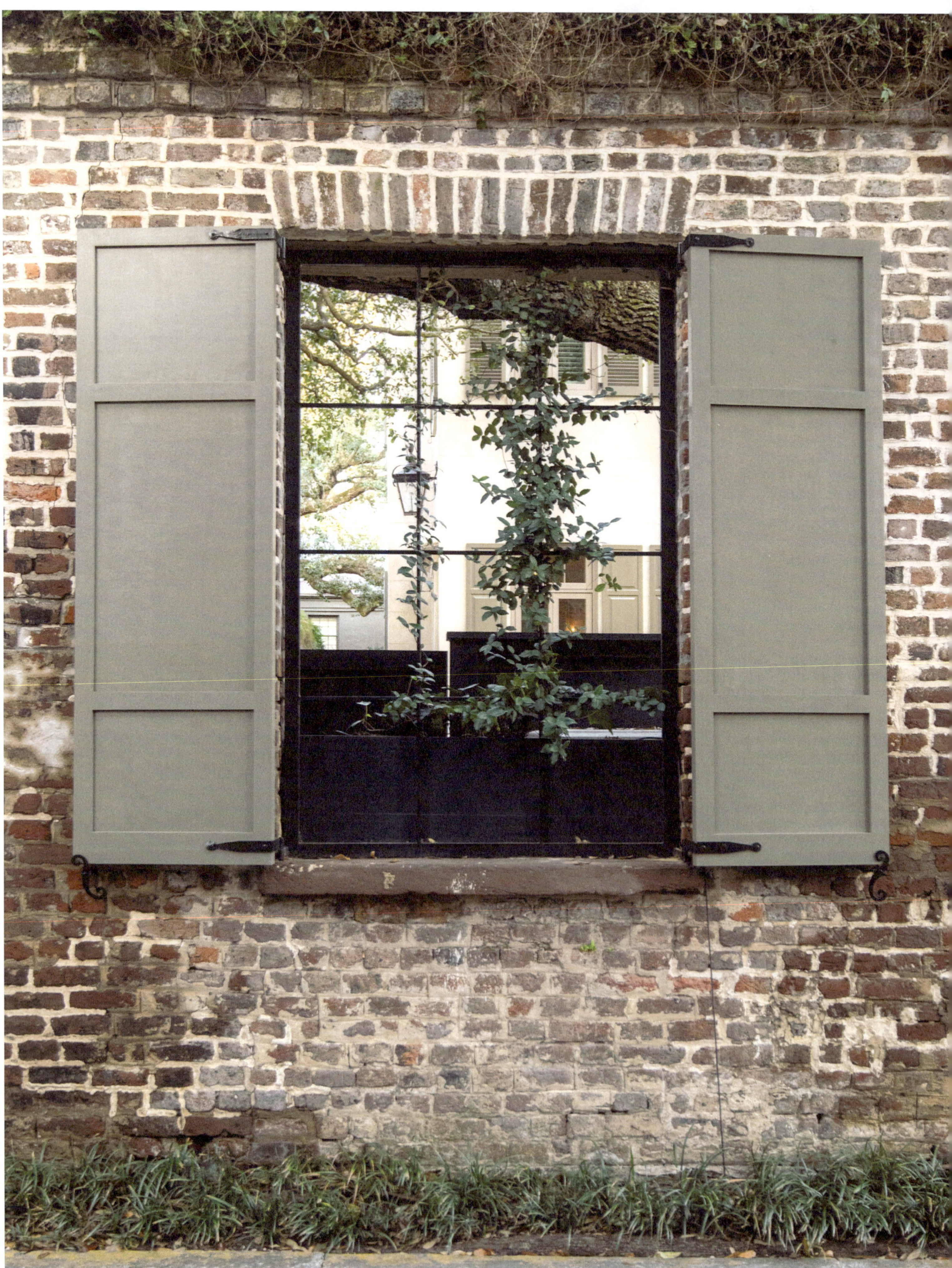

Ravenel Bridge Light Trails

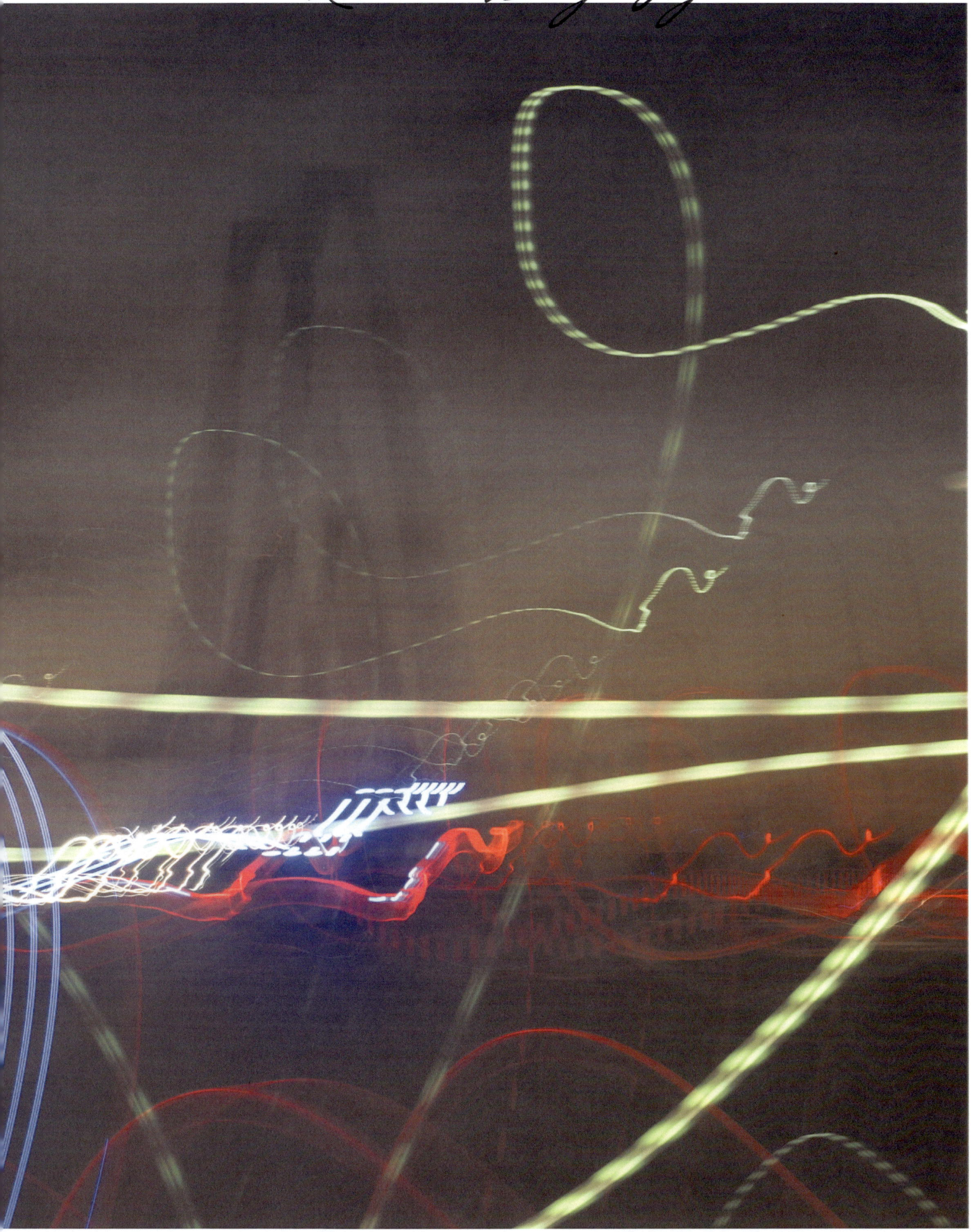

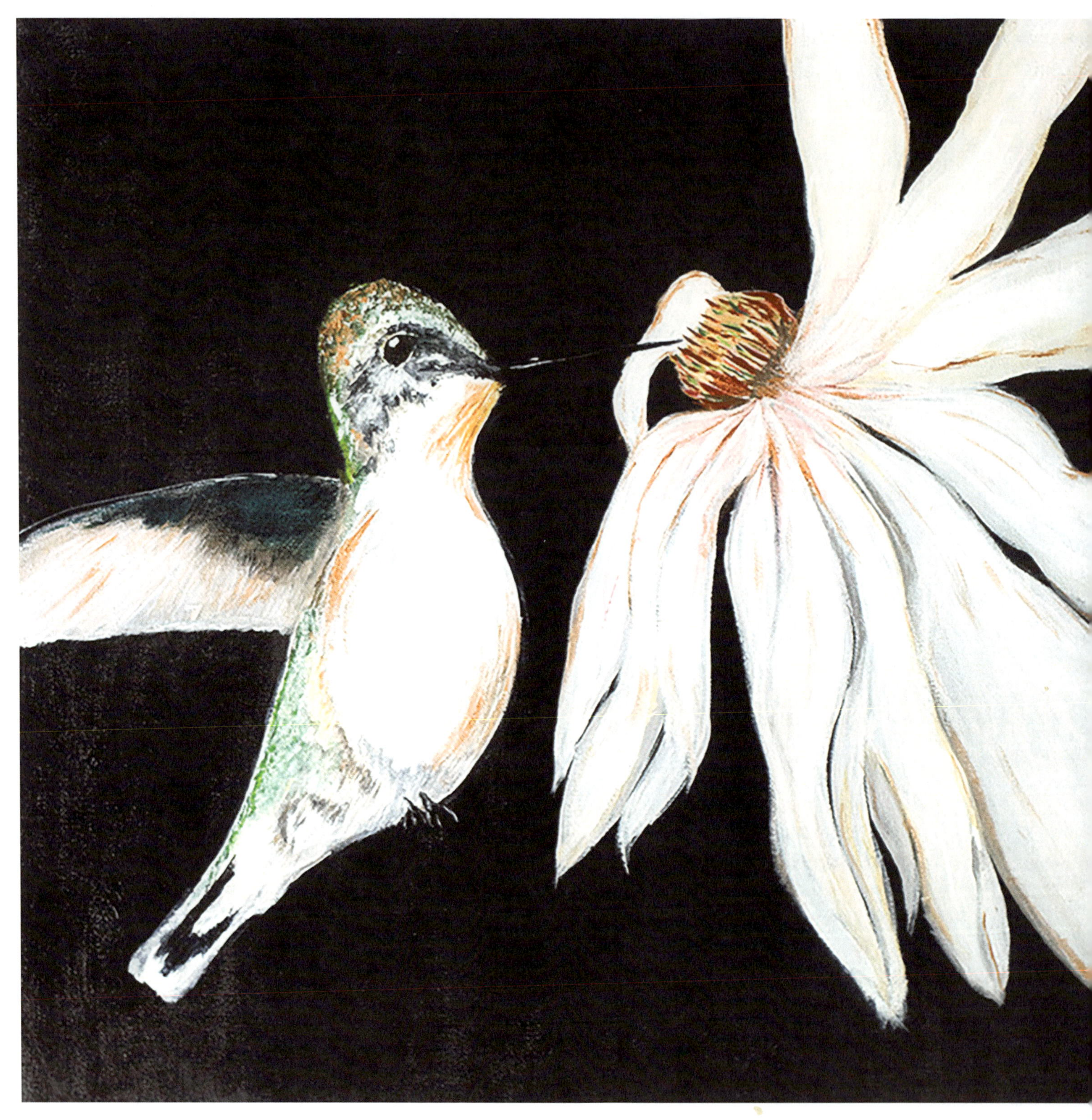

The Hummingbird and the Magnolia

20x20 acrylic on canvas

www.ingramcontent.com/pod-product-compliance
Lightning Source LLC
LaVergne TN
LVRC091029160826
845679LV00011B/1660